hey, I'm alive!

hey, I'm alive!

by Helen Klaben

WITH BETH DAY

McGraw-Hill Book Company

NEW YORK   TORONTO   LONDON

12/66 D/O Univ. BK Serv. 1.39

For my mother

There's a land where the mountains are nameless,
And the rivers all run God knows where;
There are lives that are erring and aimless,
And deaths that just hang by a hair;
There are hardships that nobody reckons;
There are valleys unpeopled and still;
There's a land—oh, it beckons and beckons,
And I want to go back—and I will.

From "The Spell of the Yukon"
by Robert Service

hey, I'm alive!

Prologue

I've only begun to live. It's too soon in my life for an autobiography. Yet I can remember wanting to write a book about my life after reading *The Diary of Anne Frank*. I was in sixth grade then and I mentioned my desire to write to my friend Linda Goldstein. She put me down with, "What ever happened to you?" I let it go at that, but I still felt my life was interesting and just as important as Anne Frank's, even if no one else thought so.

Last year, just a few short months ago, I doubt there was anyone outside my immediate family who cared who or what I was. I suppose every person in the world wants to write about himself, and just because I was in a plane crash and survived, just because I was stranded for forty-nine days in the Yukon and survived, I am lucky enough to have the opportunity to write about myself. I want to tell about everything that happened to me during those forty-nine days, but more important, I also want to try to write honestly and clearly about my life before the crash. Perhaps someone can learn something. Perhaps I can.

A lot has happened to me during the first twenty-one years of my life; whether it was good or bad, happy or unhappy all depends upon how and when I look at it. At the time, living through it, I thought of myself as deprived, abandoned, unloved even. But now I think everything that happened helped make me more responsible, self-reliant and independent.

I don't consider the crash and my survival the most important experience in my life, although, in a way, it does seem to be the most critical so far. And if I have gained any wisdom, I hope to make the most of this particular experience to benefit my future. I look at the experience gained during my lifetime and the miracle of my rescue as the culmination of childhood. A wonderful boost into adulthood. Only because of my life before the crash can I appreciate my rebirth.

I

"Helen, do you still trust me?" Ralph asked.

I was very tired and not feeling well as we sat in Ralph's hotel room in Whitehorse, Yukon Territory, Canada, waiting out the hours for the weather to clear so we could take off—whenever that would be. Two days had come and gone with flying conditions bad past Teslin. That's all I knew or cared to know about flying at the time. All I was interested in was the letter I was writing to a friend in San Francisco. I had just written, "I'll see you in San Francisco, if I ever get out of this alive." But Ralph simply could not relax, so I put my letter aside.

13

It was not the first time Ralph had asked me that question. That had been when we'd first met four evenings ago in Fairbanks, the night Ralph had come to tell me about our flight to San Francisco in his little Howard five-seater.

He had looked me over then and said, "If you don't trust me, don't go."

I had looked him over right back, relying on an instinct that so far had not failed me, and told him, "I trust you."

But now I was occupied, so to put him off I said, "No. No, I don't trust you any more."

Ralph Flores *did* look like a man a girl could trust. In his early forties, he was short and stocky with a round face, black mustache, large glasses, and a Spanish accent. My first impression had been of an intelligent, competent sort of man, and very quiet by nature. And for four days Ralph had been very silent, but now . . .

"I want to tell you something, Helen," he insisted. "Pull up a chair. I want to talk to you."

I wanted to go on with my letter, but there was something in his voice that made me obey. He was leaning on his elbow across a bed; his face was very serious. I pulled a chair over near him and waited.

"I want to tell you something," he began. "I am a lay priest in my church."

So? Ralph had already told me he was a Mormon convert, a former Catholic, married and with six children. I waited.

"I've been working up on the DEW line for eighteen months, and I have not seen my family for eight
months." Ralph looked over at me. "I have not been
alone with a woman since that time."

So what's he getting at? I wondered.

"I think of you as an instrument of temptation . . .
to test my faith," Ralph told me in all seriousness. "You
are a young, attractive girl. Yet if I came near you, I'd
lose my position in my church . . . lose the church itself."

Even though Ralph had said I was the first woman
he had been alone with in eight months I felt flattered.
No one had ever told me he'd thought of me as an instrument of temptation before. The idea of Ralph wrestling
with temptation intrigued me. I had often wondered
how priests contended with just such human feelings. I
decided it was possible for a deeply religious man, as
Ralph seemed to be, to think and talk as he did. I tried
to visualize a relationship between us. He was old
enough to be my father, but I did not need a father-
substitute any more.

"I believe you are an instrument in my life," he said
now.

Although I couldn't quite understand his words, I
had no doubt of his sincerity. "And you're probably an
instrument in mine, too," I replied. "I don't know how
or why, but just the fact that I took your plane is part of
something very meaningful." Whenever I look back on
my life I can see the interrelationship of experiences,

and I knew this flight with Ralph would be an Experience.

"I'll probably die tomorrow," I said suddenly. I don't know why I said that, for I had never had a sense of the meaning of my own death. But I did have a positive feeling that something was already happening, and that the climax to the Experience was still to come.

"No," he said quietly, as though he knew, "you won't die."

"How do you know I won't die?"

"Because I know."

"How *do* you know, Ralph?"

"God told me so," he said.

"Ralph, do you talk to God?"

"My life is guided," he said quietly.

Strangely, I had always felt the same thing myself. I tried to explain this to Ralph. "God is my friend, and I can communicate with him. You see, Ralph, I don't have to get down on my knees and pray, because He listens to me wherever I am."

But Ralph really did not understand me. "Helen, you are an instrument in my life," he said again. "My mission is to save you."

"I don't need saving. God has always been good to me."

We went on talking about religion for another hour. He spoke as eloquently as he knew how, and I recognized the old sales pitch my best friend Linda Goldstein and I used to hear from the sidewalk preachers near Times Square when we were kids. Those preachers would prophesy the End of the World, and shout, "You have no salvation without Christ as your Saviour."

"Do you mean the Indians and Chinese and all the primitive people who don't believe in Christ are damned?" Linda would ask. "Even if they're really good people?"

And when the preacher, intermittently, quoting from the Bible, would tell us they certainly were, I would pipe up, "But isn't God merciful?"

Sometimes we'd ask so many questions the preacher would close his Bible, get down off his box, pick up his American flag, and disappear down the street.

I realized Ralph had his eye on me as a possible convert from Judaism to Christianity, and I was in no mood to discuss the inconclusive subject. I felt like telling him not to bother. Finally I stopped him, saying, "I can't discuss religion with you. I don't know enough about it. There is no reason for me to be converted. We'll only argue if we keep on like this, so let's stop." I wasn't angry with Ralph. But I had a God of my own, and all Ralph's words only made me feel more confident in my own faith.

The next morning we got up and dressed and got ready to leave Whitehorse for the third time.

We finally received our clearance to leave the airport around eleven o'clock on Monday morning, February 4. Ground fog still clung to the runway, but the reports indicated the bad weather was moving north and that it should be clearer on ahead toward Fort St. John, British Columbia, 602 miles away, which was to be our next stop.

We had been at the field since eight o'clock. Ralph had been kept busy, fueling the old single-engine monoplane, shifting the load, and getting periodic weather reports. But I was getting pretty restless, hanging around in that 43-degrees-below-zero weather, bundled up in my parka and my cloth rain boots. So when Ralph came back with the eleven o'clock weather report, calling, "Come on, Helen, we're taking off," I got into the plane with him, settling myself in the copilot's seat, even though the weather looked bad—light snow was now falling—and my premonitions of the night before were with me again.

I didn't say anything, though, but chewed gum, trying to calm my nerves, and studied the airways map and radio facility chart that Ralph had given me. I had been in a small plane only once before we had started this trip together, and both the landings and take-offs still scared me. As we taxied down the runway, there was so much interference on the radio I had a hard time understanding the instructions from the tower, and I don't think Ralph heard them any better than I did, but he was the pilot. There was something about the low ceiling, and then the sort of caustic voice asking repeatedly, "Are you ready to leave? Are you ready to leave?"

Ralph gunned the engine, lifted off into the gray mist and snow, then began flying upward in a nauseatingly circular motion.

I grabbed on to the sides of my seat. "What's wrong?" I yelled over the roar of the engine. "What are you doing?"

He jerked his head up. "Have to spiral through the clouds. Get out on top."

I suppose that made sense to an experienced flyer, but it didn't settle my stomach. We kept on going around and around, and I kept on chewing my gum, thinking, "He's the pilot, he's the pilot, I trust him. I told Ralph I trusted him. He knows what he's doing."

Finally, after what I guess was only a few minutes but seemed like forever, we broke out on top of the clouds. I started breathing again.

But less than an hour later we were caught in even heavier clouds and the air had become terribly turbulent. For the next two hours we flew constantly in and out of bad weather. Then we ran into storm clouds closer and closer together so that, at last, they seemed to have closed in all around us.

"Chew your gum," Ralph called to me over the combined roar of the engine and the wind outside.

I didn't answer and I didn't look at him either. There was no point in letting him see how miserable I was. About fifteen minutes earlier I had seen Ralph switch over from one gas tank to another. I knew each tank held enough gas for about forty-five minutes' to an hour's flying time, because on our earlier flight from Fairbanks to Whitehorse Ralph had asked me to remind him when forty-five minutes had passed so he could change tanks. And I had forgotten all about it. That time before the new gas tank took hold our plane had dropped a thousand feet. Now we were on what I thought was our last tank of gas. The little black clock on the control panel said two-thirty. At three, I thought, we'll be out of gas and crash.

I couldn't think of anything to say to Ralph, so I looked down at the neatly lined red and blue and green maps in my lap, then out the window at my right. But outside everything was gray swirls. I couldn't even see our wingtip.

Now Ralph started climbing again. At 10,000 feet we still hadn't broken through and we had to come down again. We had no oxygen equipment and already the air was too thin for comfort. Two-thirty-five. Only five minutes had passed. It seemed more like five hours. Everything was slowing down, as if we were in a slow-motion movie or a nightmare.

Now Ralph was cautiously circling down through the storm clouds, trying to come out somewhere below where we could see something ... landmarks ... anything.

"Study the map," he ordered, "and see what you can find down there."

But I couldn't see anything below the plane. Just that whirling gray stuff. Suddenly, I caught a second's glimpse of thickly wooded hills and mountain slopes covered with midwinter snow. But there were no lakes, no rivers, no highways, no villages. . . . Nothing I recognized at all. Then we were closed in again. I realized we were going to crash into bleak, desolate, freezing country. Two-forty. The needle in the fuel gauge was vibrating down.

"The radio chart," Ralph shouted hoarsely.

I shoved the radio range listings before his face. He started playing with the radio control, trying to pick up the navigational beam that runs from Whitehorse to Watson Lake, Fort Nelson, on to Fort St. John. For a moment, he found it; he was on the beacon. Then it faded off. Ralph swung the plane around, trying to find the beacon again. But it was no use. It was gone.

Suddenly, a sharp draft, rising from nowhere, snatched the radio chart from my lap. Although the cabin was closed, the chart simply disappeared. We both looked for it, letting the plane bounce and skid around in the clouds almost by itself. But we never saw the chart again.

Two-fifty. Fuel tank nearly empty now. I knew Ralph was lost now, I knew he didn't know where we were. He wouldn't say we were lost and I didn't say anything to him about it. I just stared out the window and kept chewing my gum. I felt terrible about losing the chart. Just a piece of paper.

Ralph couldn't fly by instruments. He'd never had the training. He could fly on a radio beam, and we'd lost that. Or visually, and we couldn't see anything. Once more he started going up again, but he had to give up when the air became too thin for us. Two-fifty-five.

Ralph started spiraling down again. I made myself look over at him. He was working so hard. He hunched over the instrument panel, squinting through his glasses. The fuel needle indicator was almost on the bottom. I looked away. Outside, everything was the same weird grayish color. We had dropped way down again, but there was nothing.

Three. The arrow hit bottom. Well, I thought, here we go, Helen. I wanted to tell him to try a crash landing in a clearing, but decided not to. I pulled my parka around me, jerked my seat belt tight. I watched Ralph look over at the gauge, then again, as if it were in slow motion, I saw him reach over and flip a switch. It was the switch for an auxiliary gas tank. If only I had taken more interest in the plane and in flying, I wouldn't have been scaring myself to death. How do you like that! We had an extra gas tank all the time.

But nothing happened. The plane seemed to be hanging motionless in the air. I heard the engine sputter, cough, then I felt the plane drift downward.

Immediately I realized what was happening. Ralph, wanting to conserve every spoonful of fuel, had waited too long to change tanks. Just as on the day I had forgot to remind him of the time, the tank had drained dry. Ralph had explained to me four days before that the fuel lines were empty and fresh fuel had not yet filled the carburetor. And now it was happening again. "The same thing," I said to myself.

We were drifting, gliding, sailing down. Still in the storm clouds. Suddenly we broke out. About 300 feet below us I could see the tree-covered slope of a mountain. Slowly, so slowly we drifted toward it.

I think I said out loud, "Okay, Helen, here it comes." I was wondering, how do you prepare for a plane crash? Just hang on? How do you sit? Somehow I was right outside myself, feeling myself having this experience of a plane crash.

Then everything was happening very fast. Just outside the window were the trees. I saw our right wingtip hit the trees, and I guess I must have just closed my eyes. The last thing I remember thinking was, "What should I do with my feet?"

II

I opened my eyes again and looked outside, "Hey, I'm alive!" I thought. "Well, what do you know? We did crash. I was right."

I realized I was sitting in a crashed plane, but I did not understand right away that I had been blacked out for perhaps half an hour. Then before I even looked to see I felt my left arm was broken. I was surprised, and I remember thinking I had never broken a bone before in my life. My right foot was wedged between the seat and the side of the plane; I couldn't move it and it hurt. I wasn't conscious of cuts, but there was blood on the map in my lap. Then I realized my chin was split, and the right side of my face was bruised.

I looked around toward Ralph, hoping he was alive. His seat had broken loose and he was crumpled against the front of the plane. There was blood all over his face from deep cuts on his head, lips and chin. Blood was pouring out of his mouth. The baggage in back had fallen forward, breaking his seat loose, and had pushed him into the sharp edges of the instrument panel. The panel was covered with blood. It didn't look like any blood I had ever seen before. It was sort of waxy. After a moment, I realized the blood had already frozen.

It was very cold, and the first thing I thought was to get Ralph to put on his parka. He was wearing only a light jacket. As he lay there motionless and with all that blood coming out of him I was hoping against hope that somehow he was still alive.

"Ralph," I said quietly. "Ralph." Then I called his name louder. I kept calling him for almost five minutes, but I was afraid to jar him for fear he had broken bones.

Finally he began to move a little. He was very groggy, and muttered something about being sleepy and not wanting to wake up.

"Put your parka on," I told him, keeping my voice low. I didn't want to frighten him.

His lips were gouged and shredded, his chin was split, his left eye was a mass of purple and red. The blood vessels must have ruptured under the skin, so it looked as though it were filled with blood. This huge bruise extended over the eye down into the cheekbone, which looked as though it had been shattered.

"Are you okay?" I asked.

"My jaw's broken," he said. "And my ribs. How about you?"

"My arm's broken. My right foot's stuck. I can't move it."

Each of us spoke matter-of-factly, as though mutually determined not to make the other panic. Looking back on it, it's amazing how outside myself I was. My mind was sharply clear; I was acutely aware of everything, particularly the necessity not to panic. It wasn't quite twilight yet, and from a distance I saw myself figuring we would have to get out in the snow and get a fire going. I saw myself try to get out, try to move my right foot again. But it was stuck, and now I couldn't feel it.

The plane must have pitched violently when it hit the trees, because it had settled nose down and the cabin was at about a 45-degree angle. Everything had been thrown forward that had not been tied down, and the front of the plane was a shambles. Ralph decided to try to get out through the broken plexiglas windshield. I helped him get into his parka. His chest and jaw were hurting him terribly; every movement was an effort.

"I'll start a fire," he said. "You wait till I get it going."

Somehow he crawled into the back of the plane,

opened the toolbox he carried and got out a hammer and chisel. There were wrenches and pliers and things like that, but no ax or hatchet, just a hunting knife. Luckily, we had between us plenty of matches. I smoked; Ralph, being a Mormon, of course did not. His matches, he told me, had been in the plane for months.

Ralph crawled back, tried the door which was jammed shut, then started to inch his way on his belly through the shattered windshield out onto the nose of the plane. I helped him as much as I could, pushing from behind.

It was getting dark now. While Ralph was gathering wood from the trees splintered by our crashing plane, I struggled to work my right foot free. I finally got it loose. My foot was very swollen, and felt as if it had been crushed. My legs and feet were freezing.

When Ralph had a fire going, he came back for me and helped me out through the broken window. As he lifted me down into the snow, he said, "You know why we are here, don't you?"

"Why?" I said.

"Because you reject Jesus Christ."

I could hardly believe my ears—partly because Ralph could hardly move his jaws and talked with the greatest difficulty through clenched teeth, and partly because it seemed such an incredible thing to say at a time like this.

I shrugged and hobbled away from him toward the fire. I was annoyed. Why would Ralph say a thing like that—about my rejecting Christ? Why would he want to start an argument? I knew we couldn't argue; I knew we had to stick together. So I didn't say a word.

It was almost dark now. We stood around the fire trying to warm ourselves. I kept the fire going by feeding pieces of wood into it that Ralph had gathered. The night was bitterly cold. The thermometer in the plane still seemed to work. It had said 48 degrees below zero before I'd got out. There were pieces of wreckage and splintered trees scattered all around in the snow, which was pretty deep—up to our knees, and in some places to our waists. The storm we had come down in was really raging all around. Wind whistled through the tall spruce and pine trees. We both realized it would be difficult for a search plane to spot our fire and smoke through the clouds and the trees. We didn't know where we were, whether we had come down in the Yukon or British Columbia.

Whenever I got close enough to the fire really to feel it, I felt scorched. When I backed off, I started freezing again. My right foot throbbed. Finally, we struggled back to the plane.

Inside again, we tried to figure out the best way to keep warm for the night. It was hard to move things with the floor at an angle, and cold air kept rushing through the broken windshield. Ralph hung the engine cover over the opening, and then we tried to arrange ourselves on the back seat. My boots were all wet from standing around the fire in the snow. When I took the boot off my right foot to dry it, I found that the foot looked crushed.

Then I saw my big, soft-sided dress bag, which Ralph had left in the back seat. It was packed with dresses and coats. Ralph pulled out his knife and slit the case. I split it farther open, and we started pulling things out without even bothering to unfasten the catches of the suitcase.

We pulled shirts and sweaters and coats on top of us and wrapped others around our legs and feet. Since all the cuts on Ralph's face were still bleeding badly, I took one of the sweaters, a soft one, and wrapped it around his neck to keep the blood from dripping on his parka. He caught one end of the sweater between his teeth and sucked on it, trying to staunch the blood still running from his mouth. We each had hoods on our parkas, and I also had the hood to my thermal sweat-shirt. When I found the warm, fake-fur gold-colored hat I'd been wearing to work in Fairbanks, I gave it to Ralph and he put it on. It fitted down close over his head and ears.

I think we tried a million ways to sleep that night, but it was impossible to get comfortable. I couldn't stop shivering, black blisters on my fingertips were oozing, and every time I moved my arm and right foot hurt me terribly. The temperature inside the cabin seemed as cold—or colder—than it was outside the plane, despite the piles of coats and sweaters and the parkas we had on us. I was lying pressed against the side of the plane; and I never was able to get warm. Ralph was lying with his back to me in the center of the plane. He wasn't touching a side as I was, but he was just as cold. His trousers had ripped in the legs at the impact of the crash and he couldn't get his legs or feet warm.

We talked a little off and on. Ralph reminded me of my premonition of dying the night before in Whitehorse and his assurance that I would not die. He seemed to think God had placed us in this mess for reasons of His own. But Ralph was sure we would be saved. He told me to study the Bible he had along with him in the plane; that when I had accepted Christ, we would be rescued. I agreed to read the Bible. I had always intended to, anyway, but somehow had never found the time.

I asked him if he really thought anyone knew we had crashed, and Ralph said as soon as our plane was reported overdue at Fort St. John, as it surely would be the next day, an air search would begin. But, he said, it would probably be several days before we were sighted, so I would have plenty of time to study the Bible. I don't know if Ralph thought his words would reassure me, but they didn't. I felt miserable.

Ralph remembered there was a little tinned food in the plane that we had brought along for snacks, but I was too weak and sick and tired to bother. All I wanted was to sleep. Once when I did doze off for a few minutes, I woke myself, calling, "Ma, I'm alive! I'm alive!" I wanted terribly for her to know I wasn't badly hurt, for her not to worry. I guess I concentrated so hard some of it got through to her, for later she told me that on the night we crashed she dreamed I came to her bed, stood beside and spoke to her. I told her I had been "a little bit hurt" but I was "okay." My mother says her dream helped bolster her faith that I was alive all the time we were lost.

Finally, after trying every possible way to lie, we gave up and sat up, knees to knees, just waiting for daylight to come.

The next morning it got light around eight o'clock. The thermometer still said 48 below. I didn't know if that really was the temperature, or if the thermometer was broken and had got stuck there.

Ralph got up and somehow got the smashed plane door off and then covered the doorway with a tarpaulin. I just huddled under my sweaters and his parka, watching him. How anyone in his awful condition was able to do the things he did I will never know. It wasn't just Ralph's strength—although he was certainly strong enough—or even his courage—and he is the most courageous man I've ever known—but his perseverance, his refusal ever to give up, to admit anything was out of control. In the end, I guess it was his faith; his faith in himself and in God.

After Ralph got the door off, we started clearing out an area behind the back seat for what we hoped we could make into a more comfortable sleeping space. We worked at this on and off all day. It took so long because we were both weak and in considerable pain.

Ralph crawled out of the plane and, using my matches, got a fire started again. With some difficulty he made covers for my feet out of pieces of tarpaulin, mentioning as he worked that he had no feelings in his fingertips or his feet. Then, with his help I climbed out of the plane and hobbled over to the fire to get warm. I brought the blood-soaked maps along and threw them on for kindling. That may have been a mistake, for, disgusting and blotted as they were, those maps were the only things we had that ever could have shown us where we were. Ralph had made the fire five or six feet away from the plane. One of the trees he'd cut down fell near the fire, making a perfect bench. Instead of burning it, we decided to use it to sit on.

I looked around me in the early-morning gray light. We were on a mountainside in a dense spruce and pine forest. It was not actually snowing, but the little patch of sky we could see through the trees was very overcast. The only other place where I could see the sky was along the huge slash our plane had made crashing through the trees. Our wings had been shorn off right up to the fuselage. I still don't see how we both weren't killed.

We returned to the plane, and Ralph started trying to repair one of the two damaged radios on the instrument panel. I checked our supplies. We had:

4 small, flat (3¾-ounce) cans of sardines
2 7-ounce cans of tuna fish
2 1-pound cans of mixed fruit salad

1 1-pound, 8-pack box of saltines
½ bottle of protein pills
½ bottle of multi-vitamin pills
5 little pieces of chocolate
2 tablespoons of Tang (orange crystals)

We had no liquor of any kind, and I doubt Ralph would have taken it if we had, since it is against his religious beliefs to drink strong spirits—or even coffee. I had noticed when we ate together in Whitehorse he'd ordered Postum. Each of us carried some chewing gum, and I had one and a half packs of cigarettes. But I felt no desire to smoke them, and since they were dangerous around the plane anyway (I kept thinking of that full auxiliary gas tank that miraculously had not exploded during the crash), I decided this was as good a time as any to break the habit.

In addition to Ralph's tools and one box and several books of matches, we had the clothes in my suitcases, my hand mirror and a larger mirror of Ralph's, a pair of binoculars, several empty quart oil cans (and some full ones), and three small knives of Ralph's.

That was all I could find. I asked Ralph where he had stored the emergency rations and survival equipment.

"We don't have any."

"Why not?"

"They take up too much space and weigh too

much," he said, without turning around. "A lot of pilots don't carry survival equipment."

I thought that over for a minute, then asked, "Ralph, do you have any insurance?"

"No."

"But why not?"

"Insurance is too expensive; I can't afford it."

All of a sudden I became upset. I started lecturing Ralph about responsibility. I told him I wouldn't think of driving anyone in my car without insurance; it just wouldn't be fair or sensible. And an airplane was much more dangerous than a car. But when he didn't answer me I grew silent. After all, it was too late to worry and complain about those things. I didn't blame Ralph then and I don't blame him now. I took my own chances. I was just disappointed.

Soon we both became very thirsty. For water, we put snow in oil cans, set it near the edge of the fire, and as soon as it started to melt, drank it cold. It didn't taste very good, and it had sediment and twigs from the trees. I think I ate a few crackers along with the water. Poor Ralph. He couldn't open his mouth at all; he just sucked at the water.

While we were sitting there we heard what we were positive was an airplane. On and off during the morning we had been straining to hear another noise. It sounded pretty far away and somehow lower than we were, as though it might be in a valley or a lake somewhere. We'd hear it or think we heard it faintly, then it would stop. Then maybe an hour or so later we'd hear it again. Neither of us could identify the sound, although we were sure it had something to do with civilization. It sounded to me like the garbage trucks grinding garbage in the early morning a few blocks away from our house in Brooklyn.

In the afternoon, after Ralph felt he had the little radio fixed, he showed me how to work it from inside the plane. The radio was not equipped to receive, but we could broadcast. Then we heard another plane overhead. Ralph scrambled outside and started piling green pine on the fire to make smoke. He smothered and fanned the flames with his leather gloves, trying to send up signals.

I picked up the plane mike and began broadcasting, as Ralph had instructed me. "May Day. May Day. This is Howard N5886. We are alive. We hear you west. Please come back. We need medical attention and food. I am changing frequencies." Then I switched to another frequency and broadcast the same message. "We can hear you. Please come back!" Then, as I heard the engine overhead grow fainter, I called, "In the name of God, please come back."

Even as I said it, I wondered if I should. I had never said anything in the name of God before. I felt guilty somehow. But the plane didn't hear me. It flew on and was soon nothing but a hum in the distance.

There were no more planes that day.

III

"Don't cry, Helen," Ralph said.

"I have to cry, I have to cry," I sobbed.

"Helen, please don't cry."

"But I have to. Please let me cry. Please."

It was the third day since the crash, and I just couldn't stop crying. Planes kept passing overhead, but we couldn't see them through the low gray clouds and they couldn't see us or our smoke signals struggling up through the trees. I kept calling and calling to them on the radio, but they never heard me. It was still terribly cold—40 below—and dark, and my foot and arm hurt awfully. For the first time I was really hungry. I felt no one knew we were lost and alive except God, and I couldn't understand why He had put me here. I have felt for many years that everything that happens in life has a purpose, even if we can't always understand it. I feel that the life or death of a person affects other people, and I knew my mother must be terribly worried and frightened. Somehow I was sure God was punishing me or my mother for something, but I didn't know what I had done wrong, and I knew my mother couldn't have done anything wrong. So I cried.

Ralph did his best to comfort me. He said the search would go on until we were found and that my mother would have learned by now that everyone was looking for us. Then he decided to try to set my arm. Ralph fashioned rough splints out of fragments of the plane's wing, and we tore up a cotton dress of mine for bandages. Then I sat as close to the fire as I dared and peeled off a few layers of sweaters. When we got to the sweatshirt next to my skin, we decided I could push up the sleeve and hold it, without taking it off. He splinted the arm and bound it tightly; too tightly it seemed to me, for my left hand soon went numb. But even temporary numbness was an improvement over the sharp, stabbing pain with every movement that had kept me from sleep the last two nights.

We had put the two long cushions from the back seats on top of the plane carpets for mattresses and covered ourselves with all the sweaters and coats we had used the night before, plus a tarpaulin. Again we tried all sorts of sleeping positions—including one where we lay in opposite directions with my feet under Ralph's parka and his feet under mine. But nothing worked, and finally we gave up and lay side by side, shivering, dozing on and off until it grew light.

That morning Ralph had built a fire and melted snow for breakfast while I stayed in the plane huddled under the parkas and tarpaulins. His broken jaw was so painful he couldn't even swallow water. Despite his pain, Ralph dressed my injured foot with strips from one of my dresses, covered it with a sweater and made me foot coverings out of canvas and string. After that, I got back in the plane and spent the day reading, calling into the mike when a plane passed, and dozing. Ralph kept hacking away the trees with his hammer and chisel. By the time he'd cut a tree down, the stump looked as if Ralph had chewed it through.

We were still sure we were going to be rescued any minute, and so we squandered our food and ate two meals. Really, *I* ate twice. For lunch Ralph just sipped the warm juice from one of the cans of mixed fruit he warmed over the fire. I ate the whole can. The hot fruit was delicious. It reminded me of the stewed fruit compotes—prunes and apples and raisins and figs—my mother sometimes made in the wintertime. I also ate half a can of tuna fish. At dinner, I finished the tuna fish while Ralph opened a can of sardines (which I didn't like), mashed them up, mixed the mash with water and, using a twig for a spoon, got some of the mess painfully into his mouth. That night, despite or perhaps because of the food I had eaten, I was hungrier than ever and slept very badly.

As Ralph worked on my arm I looked at him and thought what messes we both were. His white shirt and leather and poplin jacket were covered with blood. The sweater I'd wrapped around his neck and jaws was already so full of blood I figured it would be due for the bonfire soon. Ralph's left eye seemed to be sinking farther into his cheek, or what was left of his cheek, which was a pulpy-looking mass. His whole face was cut and gouged and slashed, and livid with colors: blue and red. Ralph asked me several times if he looked too bad, and I always told him he didn't look bad at all. It was part of my effort to keep his spirits up. But, of course, he did the same and much more for me.

Although the cut on my chin had stopped bleeding, I, too, had blood all over me and my clothes. The blood was very bright, orangey red and looked waxy and frozen like the blood on the instrument panel. Soot from the fire settled on top of my face and clothes. I felt and looked filthy.

With my arm bound I found I could use that hand somewhat more than before. I was restricted pretty much to hobbling about in a semicircle on the side of the plane where Ralph had stomped down the snow and built a fire. Both feet were, in their sweaters and canvas coverings, more or less useless, especially the right one.

I had always been agile and well coordinated. Now I stumbled constantly. Two or three times I fell down in the snow, laughing at my own clumsiness.

The weather remained around 40 below zero all that week. We heard planes constantly, and once we even saw one in our limited patch of sky above the broken trees. But he didn't see or hear us. We still expected to be rescued at practically any moment. Sooner or later, we told each other, one of the search planes would spot our wreckage or our smoke signals, or would hear me calling to them on the radio.

From the first, Ralph did most of the physical work. He let me know I was responsible for the "housekeeping" of the interior of the plane and for keeping the fire burning after he had got it started each morning, but he did everything else, including the cooking—what little cooking there was to do. I don't know how he did everything, because his fingers and his toes were terribly swollen. He couldn't get his shoes on his feet, so he wrapped them in sweaters and put his galoshes on over them. This left him scarcely more mobile than me; yet he kept hobbling around, tearing branches off dead trees for kindling for the fire and hacking away at trees—small and large—with his hammer and chisel. He did not try to cut them into log lengths, as he did at first, but merely pulled them, tops first, into the fire with their heavier ends spread out around the flames, like the spokes on a wheel.

It was my job, once the end had burned, to drag the next section into the fire. At the time we crashed, I had been wearing cotton dress gloves with woolen gloves pulled over them. Within the first few days I had managed to burn both pairs, handling the scorched wood. I threw the gloves into the fire and put on the other pair I had found in my suitcase, and pulled wool socks on over them. Ralph wore my wool socks on his hands and feet.

My worst problem continued to be balance. Once, while I was tending the fire, I leaned forward to pull a section of tree into it, stumbled and fell into the fire. I pulled myself up, and looked down in astonishment to see flames shooting up from my canvas-covered feet, Without really thinking, I lunged from the fire into a snowbank. I was too embarrassed at my own clumsiness to call Ralph for help. Later, when he saw the holes in my canvas foot covers Ralph scolded me. "Don't get so close to the fire, Helen," he said. "We haven't that much canvas."

Since it was difficult for me to walk, I worried about not getting any exercise. I had been really overweight when I'd left Fairbanks, weighing about 140 pounds, and even with all this forced dieting I didn't think I'd lost much. Since I was sure we were about to be rescued and I wanted to look good when we got out of there, I started doing setting-up exercises, hanging on to a tree. The first day all I could do was five kneebends. I worked up to fifteen before I quit. But mostly I stayed inside the plane.

We kept trying to make our existence more comfortable inside the cabin by stuffing extra clothes into all the cracks we could find and making a kind of blanket out of the carpet from the plane and insulation from the ceiling. Ralph chiseled off a bar between the rear seat and the luggage compartment, so we could stretch out better at night. He tried to repair things, the radios, the airplane clock and his self-winding wrist watch. My watch, which I wore on my left arm, had been smashed when my arm was broken. We found the watch on the floor of the plane—in several pieces.

Ralph set up his mechanic's tool chest alongside the plane, and one day I noticed he had covered the chest with my two favorite dinner dresses: a black silk tunic lined with red satin, and a flowered pink sheath with a portrait neck. When I inquired about my dresses, he just said, "The snow won't hurt 'em," and kept right on working.

I wasn't fully convinced, but I didn't think to exchange them with something else until some days later. Besides, Ralph had an authority about him that I respected. More and more he was treating me like one of his own children. Sometimes it irked me, but most of the time I found it oddly comforting. He had twin sixteen-year-old daughters who were getting ready for college, and I think Ralph lumped me in their age bracket.

After the first few days, I noticed he occasionally called me "Daughter" as well as "Helen"—in fun at first, and then it became a habit. I tried to call him "Daddy" in return, but it didn't sound right somehow, and I still couldn't really quite think of Ralph as a father. But he was certainly acting like one toward me, ordering me around, looking after me, fussing at me sometimes—just as he would one of his own kids. I decided to call him "Daddy-O." It was meant in a joking way, but it was also affectionate.

Although Ralph was never exactly loquacious, he was most talkative in the mornings over our "breakfasts." Curiously, we hardly ever talked at night in the cabin. Just "Goodnight, Helen," "Goodnight, Ralph," then the long, freezing, fretful hours until dawn. One night I dreamed of our rescue in detail. In my dream it was a helicopter that came for us. It hovered over our camp, and a long extension cable was let down. I was in our plane when I heard the helicopter and I jumped out and limped over to the cable. Then I paused, wondering what I should take back with me.

After that dream, I kept watching for a helicopter. It had been so convincing I was sure that was how we would be taken out. I also figured that when we were rescued we'd first be flown back to Whitehorse, then flown on home from there. I realized I needed medical care of my arm and foot, and I visualized myself greeting my family on crutches, with my arm in a cast.

I had been too rushed leaving Fairbanks to get

souvenirs for the family. Now I thought a lot about what I could get them when we went back to Whitehorse. We talked most about our families. I tried to think of things to amuse Ralph; stories, riddles, jokes, but I could never remember any except several slightly risqué jokes I had heard at the office in which I had worked in Fairbanks, and I certainly couldn't tell those to Ralph. So I just talked about my mother and my four brothers and two sisters.

Ralph told me about his children. He was planning to send the sixteen-year-old twins to Brigham Young University in Utah. Next in age to them was a fifteen-year-old boy; then there was a ten-year-old girl, another boy, and a little girl. His wife's parents still lived in Mexico, where Ralph also originally came from, and he told me about meeting his wife in San Francisco, where she was living with an aunt and uncle. He told me about asking their permission to marry Teresa and of their life together after their wedding. Ralph made his wife and children seem very real and wonderful to me, and he, in turn, soon felt he knew my mother, since I spoke so often of her.

Outside of a mutual love of our families, I guess we were about as far apart as people could be. Ralph was simple, extremely serious, withdrawn. He told me he didn't enjoy the things that most people did: dancing and drinking and playing poker and being gay. He said that the other men he worked with always thought he was odd because he didn't drink or play around. He didn't even swear. He said it had been like that all his life. He was never popular because he wasn't fun to be with; he was too quiet.

Since the intense cold and my injuries kept me inside the plane a good deal of the time, I started reading. Ralph always carried religious books with him wherever he went, and he had a small trunk full of them. But I didn't get into them because I had enough of my own that I wanted to read. I had a copy of the prose and poems of Robert Service, the "poet laureate of the Yukon," that I had bought in Whitehorse; also the complete paperback nine-volume Great Books course in a cardboard case that I had been studying in Fairbanks. I had already read and discussed some of them in class, but the others I wanted to read now, particularly the selections from Thoreau and Tolstoy. We also had up front Ralph's Bible and a children's book of his called *The Birthday of Jesus Christ*.

The first thing I read was the Gospel according to St. Matthew, which was one of the Great Books. I read some of it aloud to Ralph, and we talked about it, but weren't able to discuss it as I would have liked. We were still engaged in our battle of wills about my accepting Christ. Ralph certainly felt it was his mission to make me accept his faith. He also thought that if one Jew converted, maybe more Jews would be hospitable to Christianity. He seemed to feel that Jews were pretty withdrawn and clannish, and the world would be better off if they opened their hearts to Christianity.

I didn't reject Christ. I just didn't see why people had to believe he was divine. To me, he was a great personality and teacher, a great prophet and leader like Moses and Mohammed, with tremendous appeal to the poor and needy, as well as to people of all faiths and beliefs. But when I said those things, Ralph was practically beside himself with anxiety. He seemed to think I *must* believe—because he told me to. He even had an idea we would not be rescued until I recognized Christ.

"Did I ever tell you anything wrong?" he said. "Did I ever tell you to do anything that wasn't right?"

"No, you haven't," I said.

"Then why don't you accept Jesus Christ when I ask you to?"

I tried to reason with him. "When I get home I'll study religion," I promised. I had always intended to study comparative religion in college.

"It isn't what you learn, Helen. It comes through the heart."

"But there's so much in the Bible I don't understand," I said. "I'd like to go to a good university and study the Bible and learn what these things really mean."

Ralph shook his head firmly. My approach did not make sense to him. To his way of thinking, if I accepted the fact that he was a good man, then I ought also to accept his faith—without question. I tried to explain to him that I had to find my own way into religion the same as I did anything else. I could not accept blindly. I did admit to an ignorance of the Bible, especially the New Testament, which I had never read, and I promised Ralph I would try to read all of it.

At first, I read the Bible out loud to Ralph, but I quit since I read faster to myself and skimmed over such parts as the "begats" of Genesis. I'd read the Bible a while, then pick up Service or Thoreau or Tolstoy, and read a little out loud from them. But Ralph wasn't interested in literature. Whenever he saw or heard me switching from the Bible he protested.

"Stay with the Bible," he said over and over. "You must finish it."

"But these are good books, too," I said. "They're not trash."

Despite Ralph's feelings, I continued to dip into the selections from *Walden*. I didn't care much for the long descriptive passages when Thoreau was talking about ponds and trees and summer, because we didn't have a beautiful pond and fresh fish to eat or even much sky to see, and it wasn't summer. We just had a lot of snow and uninteresting trees, and after a while that gets pretty depressing. Thoreau had an ax, and we didn't even have that. But I did like the parts where he philosophized on life: the idea that so long as you had your own mind, your own thoughts, you need never be bored or forsaken. I underlined:

Direct your eye right inward and you'll find
a thousand regions in your mind
Yet undiscovered . . .

Then I read Tolstoy's "The Death of Ivan Ilych," which impressed me as the best short story I had ever read. In the story, Ivan Ilych, when he is dying, looks back on his life. That started me looking back on mine. I reflected on all the things I had done—good and bad—and I began to think about how each event in my life was related to another event and experience, and how this long chain of events and experiences, starting with my childhood in Brooklyn, had somehow mysteriously led me to Alaska and now to a plane crash and this strange life with Ralph in the wilderness.

IV

. . . Dear Mother, I love you so much. Please don't worry.
I'm really O.K. Ma, I'm all right. I wish you were here
with me, comforting me. I'd curl up just like a baby,
with my head resting against your breast. You're so
warm and soft. You were always so warm and soft. Oh
Ma, I wish I were with you again. I'll take very good care
of you. Don't ever worry. Please God, don't punish my
mother. She is too good.

Thank you for the beautiful sweater you sent for
my birthday. It's so nice and warm. I wore it only on
special occasions. Now I keep it under my head when I

try to sleep rather than on my shivering feet. Oh Ma, I'm not crying because of the cold, I'm not crying because I'm hungry or because my feet throb. I just want to be with you. I'm so filled with tears they just about freeze in my eyes.

Please, I'm sorry for all the times I yelled at you, and gave you nothing but abuse for your trouble. I took everything out on you because I loved you so much. I was so sure of your love for me. God, please give me a chance to make it up to her. Thank you, my wonderful God, for such a wonderful mother. Thank you again for giving me the chance to appreciate her once again. My mother is beautiful, and as far as I can see, she deserves only good. She has brought good to so many people, and has only suffered in return. Her biggest fault is being too good....

Thinking about my mother so fervently led me naturally back to the Bible and the First Book of Samuel, for I was named after my mother's mother Hannah (in Jewish families children are often named after a relative by the initial letter only instead of the whole name). In the Bible, Hannah is the mother of Samuel, the father of Saul. After the birth and weaning of Samuel, Hannah offered this song of thanksgiving to the Lord:

And Hannah prayed and said, My heart rejoiceth in the Lord, mine horn is exalted in the Lord; my mouth is enlarged over mine enemies; because I rejoice in thy salvation.

There is none holy as the Lord: for *there is*

none beside thee: neither *is there* any rock like our God.

Talk no more so exceeding proudly; let *not* arrogancy come out of your mouth: for the Lord *is* a God of knowledge, and by him actions are weighed.

The bows of the mighty men *are* broken, and they that stumbled are girded with strength.

They that were full have hired out themselves for bread; and *they that were* hungry ceased: so that the barren hath born seven; and she that hath many children is waxed feeble.

The Lord killeth, and maketh alive: he bringeth down to the grave, and bringeth up.

The Lord maketh poor, and maketh rich: he bringeth low, and lifteth up.

He raiseth up the poor out of the dust, *and* lifteth up the beggar from the dunghill, to set *them* among princes, and to make them inherit the throne of glory: for the pillars of the earth *are* the Lord's, and he hath set the world upon them.

He will keep the feet of his saints, and the wicked shall be silent in darkness; for by strength shall no man prevail.

The adversaries of the Lord shall be broken to pieces; out of heaven shall he thunder upon them: the Lord shall judge the ends of the earth; and he shall give strength unto his king, and exalt the horn of his anointed.

Although I had read Hannah's song of thanksgiving many times before, it was as if I had now come upon it for the first time, so fresh and powerful and meaningful it seemed to me.

My grandmother died almost two years before I was born. My grandmother had been a widow since my mother was thirteen. She came from Austro-Prussia, and my grandfather from Poland during the pogroms. They met and were married in this country. The pictures of her show a soft and tender face; very understanding and wise eyes. Eyes that have known heartache and struggle; eyes very much like my mother's. My mother never burdened her children with the hardships of her childhood, or lack of childhood. She learned to take suffering in her stride and not contaminate those around her. She is all the Ethel Waters characters rolled into one.

After four boys, one girl, and a lapse of five years, I was born. At least, I was a girl, and that made things nice, since my mother wanted another girl. Twenty months later she gave birth to another girl. When there's a will, there's a way of making ends meet. Often the ends had to be stretched to the bursting point to meet, but we managed. And we were proud. We owned our own house, a two-family, semi-detached in Bensonhurst, a middle-class section of Brooklyn.

I was so happy the first five years of my life. I was a very pretty baby, so they say, and never was a bother. My mother would leave me in front of the house in my playpen. The passers-by would keep me occupied all day long. I was a big attraction in the family, with my pudgy cheeks and platinum hair, already walking at nine months. I was a novelty, but it soon wore off when Linda was born. We were the "kids" of the family. Linda was my first playmate. We were dressed as twins, and expected to do things together.

Even though we were always arguing and fighting among ourselves, we were a close-knit bunch in our own way. That made seven different ways. Marty—twelve years older than I—tried to boss us kids. Eddie told us Brer Rabbit and Uncle Remus stories, impersonating their speech. Marty and Eddie would let us sneak to the basement during their parties and take some candy and soda upstairs. Robby was the quiet organizer.

My domain included all the secret passages between, around and above the semi-detached houses on our street. "Our Gang" used the old wooden milk boxes as fortresses and all the spare wood we could find in the neighborhood as supports. We carved, hammered and nailed sticks into swords and rifles. We had the best dirt patches and gutters for marbles and, as we grew older, the best alleys for punch ball. I could do whatever I wanted whenever I wanted, just as long as I didn't cross the street without asking.

With four older brothers and a block full of boys, I had no other choice but to do as well as, if not better than, they, or be friendless except for some sissy girls, who played jump rope all day long. I was lucky to have the coordination to excel as one of the boys. I often wondered what I would grow up to be—a girl or a boy. The neighbors weren't too sure either. I was usually in a tree, trying to show the boys how to climb as high as me. I was fiercely protective of Linda, and I'd beat up anyone who picked on her, although I didn't offer her much companionship myself. Linda was not a tomboy like me. She was a sweet, loving, feminine little girl, but I was too full of myself to give her the attention she deserved.

I was going to be a cowgirl when I grew up—just like Annie in *Annie Get Your Gun*. I'd be fearless and shoot any bad critter that got in my way. I'd have my own horse and jump on and off him all day. I'd be just like Snow White when I'd go off into the woods. All the ferocious animals would come and eat out of my hand, the dewy-eyed deer would lick my face and the birds would serenade about my shoulders. And when I was in the jungle, I'd swing from vine to vine with Tarzan. The tigers and lions would be my friends and the elephants and parrots would signal if there were some trouble. I'd always take care of them; they liked me.

Since I had never had a horse, I thought it was important to buy one, keep it in my garage and ride him to school—when I went to school. I had practiced in my dreams all these years, so when I was eighteen and for the first time had an opportunity to go riding at a dude ranch, I took the intermediate trail instead of the beginner's, and did very well on it. The only difficulty was mustering up enough courage to go near the horse, because, in spite of all my dreams, I am afraid of animals. All animals. Once on board, I did all right.

I am ashamed to admit that—for no conscious reason—I cross the street if I see a dog or even a cat in my path. All my imagined bravery gets me nowhere, and I am actually scared of insects. I cringe and shut my eyes tight and scream for someone to come and kill the beetle or cockroach. It's a good thing I didn't see any animals at the crash site except those rabbits. If there was anything bigger around, Ralph was wise not to tell me about them.

I had looked forward to school. Little did I know it would open up a whole new world. There were lots of kids I never knew. They never seemed terribly interested to know me. They weren't as warm and friendly as the kids on the block. That bothered me to the point of continual introspection. I didn't have as nice dresses, and I wanted my hair in banana curls like the other girls. Everyone had pinched my chubby cheeks, patted my blond, curly hair and bestowed upon my swelled little ego all the attributes of the most beautiful, charming, active, adorable child. But when I got to school I saw I wasn't even pretty.

I was just a little bit above an average student, in the upper one-fourth of the class, excelling only in recess because I was the best punch-ball player. Starting in the third grade, I suffered from severe headaches caused perhaps by the strain and arguments at home. It was decided my headaches came from poor eyesight, so I had to wear reading glasses. I never felt like wearing them. I'd let the glasses get dirty and never washed them. I remember one teacher made me wear my glasses all day long, even though they were necessary only for reading, movies and television (we *did* have the first TV set on the block). I gradually gave up wearing my glasses (they didn't seem to affect my headaches one way or the other) until I got to college and started reading a great deal.

In grade school I never was really popular. In fact, I desperately needed a comrade-in-arms, a confidante, supporter, admirer, ego-booster. In short, I needed and wanted a girl friend. My preschool friends had been all boys except for my little sister. I still felt like one of the boys, but how would it look if I were on their side when they teased the girls?

Fortunately, I did find a girl friend—Linda Goldstein. Linda was in my fourth-grade class and lived nearby. She was better off than me, very smart, and given tap-dancing lessons, piano lessons, and all sorts of other luxuries. Linda and I shared the most complementary relationship a psychologist or a novelist could think of. We were opposite from the word go. I envied her advantages. She envied my freedom, self-reliance and my ability to excel in sports. Oh, how I wanted to take dancing and piano lessons.

If only my mother cared enough to yell after me out the window, "Helen, come in for dinner," "Helen, don't do that," "Helen, don't climb the tree, you'll get hurt," as all the other mothers on the block did. But she never did. So I felt she didn't love me. No one loved me. They didn't care if I lived or died. Maybe they would be happy if I died. One less mouth to feed. Times were hard. Money became more scarce; the arguments at home became louder.

For some reason or other, I was enrolled in Talmud Torah. My brothers had all been Bar-Mitzvahed, although at home there was no particular religious atmosphere. I knew I wasn't required to be Baz-Mitzvahed, and I didn't have any strong feelings about it. I went to Hebrew school, anyway, with all the boys in the neighborhood, and cut up in a disrespectful manner just as much as they did.

Hebrew school did instill a big question mark in my mind about religion in general. Although I didn't understand the purpose of religion, I had respect for the belief of others. One incident that hurt me personally, and made me realize I was Jewish, took place when I was seven or eight years old. There was an Italian girl on the block about the same age as I, attending parochial school. We had the habit of arguing and fighting most of the time. I could beat her up with one hand tied behind my back, and was usually ahead when we fired questions at each other to see who was smarter. In all her humiliation, she would inevitably attack me as being a dirty Jew and accuse me of killing Jesus Christ. I told her how stupid she was, since I wasn't even there, and I was sure it wasn't the Jews; it was the Romans.

The only distinction I knew that existed between people was that if you weren't Jewish, you were Italian —and you were able to tell by the last name. If it ended in a vowel, you were Italian—except in the case of Shapiro.

I always enjoyed going to *schul*. My father was treasurer. He would take Linda and me. We would walk very proudly on either side of him to the *schul* where he was a big shot and able to do anything he wanted and knew all the people. Besides, they always had candy or flags or stories for the kids there. When I got older and no longer fitted in with the kids that ran around the *schul*, I, following the example of the older women, would socialize outside, while the men were inside praying. I understood the meaning of *Yom Kippur* and *Rosh Hashana,* and couldn't understand what I took to be the hypocritical attitude of some of the congregation. It reminded me of the time I went to confession with some friends, and they would admit to the same sins week after week, yet felt absolutely secure because of the priest's absolution and blessing.

I had always wanted to pray, but I never knew how. I remember making a serious attempt by using a prayer-book, reading passages that suited my feelings, which were of repentance at the time of *Yom Kippur,* and trying to keep up with the cantor. I seemed to have finished before everyone else. When I went outside, I learned everyone else had been saying prayers for the dead. That left me with a funny feeling. I didn't know anyone who had died. I did feel I had made an honest attempt to communicate with God, even though it was at the prescribed time.

When we became more aware of religious differences, Linda Goldstein and I defended our faith and also sought to find answers to controversial religious questions, such as: was the Virgin Mary really a virgin, the possibility of salvation of non-Christian believers, the purpose of preaching to and damning everyone on street-corners, and who or what was God all about?

My mother and father separated when I was nine. More correctly, my father left home. Money, after that, was even scarcer. My mother, who rarely expresses her emotions, never complained, nor would she accept charity from our relatives. She simply found a job and worked. My three older brothers, Marty, Eddie, and Robby, helped take over. They all contributed to supporting the family and keeping the family together.

I was more on my own than before, although my older sister Ruth took care of Linda and me as much as she could. I wanted so much to have a father. It was the most important thing in the world to me. I felt everyone else had a father, and I should too. I felt there was an opening in the circle of our family; one of the links was gone. I wanted someone to take care of me, to tell me what to do. My brothers tried to be father-substitutes, but they weren't kidding me. I wanted a real father.

I remembered when I was like everyone else, when

I had a father. Linda and I would fight to see who would sit next to him at dinner. It was just like on television, a whole family. We would all talk at once, my father at the head of the table, like a king ruling a court. I guess I called him "Daddy." I remembered when he would come home, we would run up to him, Linda and I, and he would unlock the chifforobe and give us each a Hershey bar. I was sure the chifforobe was full of Hershey bars. After my father left home, many of the neighbors tried to milk Linda and me for gossip. "Where is your father?" "What does he do?" "Do you miss him?" "Where's the family's money coming from?"

It was from the example of these people that I made vows never to be like them and hurt others. I was hurt; I had nothing but the bare necessities of life. My pride was crushed under the weight of insecurity and inferiority. Deep inside, I knew I was beautiful, even though no one else could see it. Deep inside, I knew I was special, even though no one else realized it. Deep inside, I knew I had been blessed by God, even though no one else but God and I understood it. Someday, I told myself, everyone else will realize my value and beauty and goodness. I see now that all those hurts and insecurities I thought I suffered in my childhood have only made me stronger and more independent. I see now that because I thought I was ignored and reviled I built up protective shields around myself.

In junior high school I had a very difficult time

making the adjustment from a tomboy to a girl. It was around that time I began to try to analyze myself and others.

I wasn't sure what was expected of me. Around me was a cage. I wasn't sure who built the cage. I would watch others and try to understand. What was it that made others popular? If only I had the formula. It couldn't be clothes. Susan wore the same thing every day, and still Mary Anne was her best friend and Joseph C. and Joseph G. were her boy friends. Maybe it was because she lived on 77th Street. That's where Gloria and Marie lived. They like Susan, and if I lived on 77th, they would probably be my best friends, too. But Katherine is smart and has nice clothes and she is a good punch-ball player. I'm a good punch-ball player, too. Everyone likes Katherine. Susan isn't so smart. And Anna is beautiful. I didn't think the teacher liked me. She knows I'm poor. She has my brother and sister. Still, I'm not as poor as Lucy.

My first sense of belonging to a clique was in the eighth grade. Beverly and Thea and I were the only "hip" girls in our homeroom class. We weren't "creeps." We knew what it was all about. I had all the confidence as long as it was "we three," although I didn't always feel a part of the three. I never was able to afford to collect crew-neck sweaters or crinolines. And I felt silly and awkward carrying a pocketbook.

In high school we drifted apart, and I was alone

again. Although I had many "friends," I never did find my niche. I wanted to be on top and wouldn't settle for less, so I drifted—a loner. I didn't make my first rush to a sorority, because I couldn't think of one good reason why I should be accepted or what I could offer to the sorority. The expected answer was, of course, that I contribute with zeal my whole self and try to make the sorority the best sorority. After all, I thought, the fact that I was willing to undergo hazing should be proof in itself of my sincerity, of my desire for their friendship. Anyway, I made it the next term, after reciting the humbling phrases. This episode did awaken in me the realization of the importance of mutual contribution in any relationship. I understood then that, aside from just myself, I didn't have anything interesting to offer. And I didn't know exactly what I wanted in return.

In my senior year at high school I wrote a poem called "Loneliness." Some of the lines, I realize now, are terribly revealing. ". . . Boys and girls laughing and un-worried/ Can set my heart a-rage/ What am I doing here/ Without a friend to speak/ A kindly word . . ." I see now I was lost, lonely and directionless. I took everything personally and thought people were persecuting me, making cutting remarks about me, although I knew this was not actually the case. I didn't start dating regularly until I was sixteen years old, but even then I didn't find the companionship that I craved so much with boys any more than I had with girls. All the boys at school wanted to go steady and have necking partners, but I didn't want to go steady just yet. I wanted to get to know all sorts of different boys and find out what they were like.

I worked summers from the time I was fifteen. Years before, Linda Goldstein and I had wanted to work in the library. We would go there almost every day when we were in summer school and beg the head librarian for a job, or at least to let us help put the books away. No, we weren't old enough. Besides, we were becoming nuisances. We wanted at least a pre-teen card to enable us to take out books from the Junior Adult section. I never did become a librarian. By the time I was old enough, I wanted to get out in the world and see what it was all about.

I had always enjoyed taking care of babies on the block for as long as I can remember. At twelve I had a steady baby-sitting job every Saturday night for my aunt's neighbor. This was a forty-five-minute bus ride away. I slept over at night and got $2. I derived a tremendous sense of self-sufficiency from earning my own money. I had always been an independent spirit—if only by force of circumstances—and now I felt I was really on my own. I liked not having to connive to extract money from my family. Instead, my brother Arthur—then in college—used to ask me to lend him a few dollars to take a girl on a date.

I wanted to get a regular job the summer after my sophomore year in high school. But I was fifteen and a half years old, and no one wanted to hire me. Most didn't want to be bothered with getting me working papers; others said they weren't interested in summer help. Neighborhood friends were going away for the summer, and others were taking lockers at Coney Island or Brighton Beach. I couldn't afford a locker and—sour grapes, naturally—I told myself I didn't want to waste a summer at the beach.

The only alternative was lying or, as my mother put it, "white lying." Finally, after much trial and error, I figured out the most airtight employment application: I was eighteen, didn't need working papers; graduated from high school with an academic diploma (since I didn't have the secretarial skills for a commercial diploma and was too proud to admit to a general diploma); was going to night college because I couldn't afford to go in the daytime; wanted a full-time permanent position; gave my brother Robby as a reference for previous summer employment.

With this spiel I got a job with a mail-order pen-and-pencil company. I was to check their mailing list (every business in the country), using telephone books. My boss, aware of my disinterestedness and inefficiency, sent me on errands. I was happy to get out of the factory and deliver his stocks and bonds to his broker or have his watch fixed. When he laid me off after just six weeks, he told me he had only wanted temporary help anyway, and then suggested that I continue high school.

That first job—if nothing else—gave me confidence.

With a month of summer to go before school started, I got another job. On the quality of some art samples and also some bluffing, I entered—"through a side door"— the advertising world. I was a color separationist in preparing art work for going to press. That Christmas I worked in a department store, trying to look busy when there was nothing to do. The next summer I had a ball with a job as a trainee at the American Photographic Company, coloring photographs. So every vacation and every summer until I graduated from high school I worked at various jobs. I did all sorts of things. I taught ice skating in Central Park, I worked at Macy's, I coded IBM cards, I was a counselor at a summer camp, a receptionist, a bookkeeper, and lots of other things.

When I finished high school, I thought I'd like to go to college full-time, but my brother Marty, who was the head of the family, thought I should contribute some money to the family budget, as my older brothers and sister Ruthie had done. I had been accepted at City College and, in the summer, started studying nights. In the morning, I attended classes at the Arts Students League; in the afternoon I went to one job or another; and in the evening, I went to class. The two hours I had off between my art school and job I usually spent in much-loved Central Park.

That fall, the fall of 1959, I had saved enough money to go to college during the day, which I did until the fall of 1960. Although I liked college and engaged in numerous activities, I didn't really study or devote myself to it. I was terribly lazy, and was eating and sleeping too much. My Psychology 1 class encouraged me to apply all sorts of terms and jargon to my "condition." I wrote papers about how miserable I was and how terrible my childhood had been, but writing it all out didn't make me feel any better or more directed. If anything, I felt increasingly restless, rootless and disembodied.

So I left City College and went to work full-time. I started at an advertising agency where I even had a title: "assistant traffic and production manager." But what I really wanted was some kind of work in the agency's art department, and when I found out that it might take years for me to get such a job, I left and went to work for an art studio where I was assistant production manager and right back at controlling traffic again, even though I did get a ten-dollar raise.

I stuck with that job until the company went out of business. Then I got a new job with a magazine publishing company where my title was "assistant editorial production manager." Actually, though, I didn't do any more glamorous or important work than I had before. So I kept looking around and changing jobs. The last one I had was with a photographic stock-picture agency that dealt mostly with fashion pictures. I rather enjoyed the work; I had much more responsibility than ever before. But the agency's main office was in Detroit, and the communications between there and New York were poor, and finally the old office routine began to bore me again. So . . . I got a raise on a Tuesday, and resigned on a Wednesday.

Soon after that, my restlessness flared up again, and almost before I knew it, I was on my way to Alaska by car. I remember two things about my departure very clearly: my mother, trying to look happy and determined not to cry; and my sister Linda, who was not speaking to me. Linda and I had been fighting on and off for days. Nothing very serious, just the way sisters sometimes go on at each other. After a few days it had seemed easier for us not to speak. As the car pulled away, I had a sudden impulse to lean out the window and call goodbye to Linda. But I didn't.

V

I woke myself on the tenth day after the crash thinking
about Linda and about my indifference toward her ever
since we were children. Momentarily, I was convinced
my fate rested in Linda's hands. If she could forgive me
for the way I'd always treated her, if she could love me
instead of hating me, I thought I would be all right.
"Linda," I thought over and over, "please love me.
Don't hate me, Linda. Don't ask for my rescue. Just love
me!"

That day our food ran out. The last thing we ate
was the sardines and crackers. I had never liked sardines

and I had refused to share them with Ralph until they were all that was left. To my surprise, they tasted delicious, and I was sorry I had refused the other three tins that Ralph had eaten.

Several days earlier, Ralph and I had started to experiment with our water supply. Since there was a good deal of sediment from the trees in the melted snow, the water did not taste fresh when we merely let the snow sit in an oil can beside the fire till it melted. We found that if we melted a small amount of snow, then kept adding more till the can was full, and then let that water boil for a few minutes and strained it through a piece of one of my torn-up dresses, and finally reboiled the water again, the result was a warming, good-tasting beverage.

On the seventh day I had made a real discovery: two small chicken legs in the luggage compartment. They were all that remained of a frozen fried chicken we had bought in Fairbanks to eat on our flight to Whitehorse, but they were good for a whole day's food for the two of us. And I mean good! Ralph cut the chicken up into little pieces and, with our new-found skill in water-boiling, made a half-gallon of delicious soup.

On the ninth day we were down to the last of the saltines, Ralph's protein pills, and the second and last can of fruit cocktail. We heated this can, as we had done the first. I am ashamed to admit I was so hungry that I actually hoped Ralph would only be able to sip the juice, as he had done before. But his jaw was enough improved so that he could eat as much of the warm fruit as I did.

On the eleventh day I started on Ralph's protein pills. But that afternoon my feet became suddenly much more painful and blistered than they had been before. Ralph decided there must be some relationship between the pill and the blisters, so neither of us took any more of the pills, although I now realize those pills could have given us a little more strength that we were to need so desperately later. I realize now the protein pills could not have had any connection with what was happening to my foot. Strange, the things people think and do during times of extreme stress and tension. Before our life together in the wilderness was ended we were to think and do many such things.

On the twelfth day I had an attack of stomach pains that doubled me over. I was in such agony that Ralph tried to help me by patting my back and trying to burp me like a baby. Finally, the severe cramps subsided. I didn't know what had caused it, but I thought, "Maybe I'm starving to death. Maybe this is what it feels like." Yet I was still almost as fat as the day we crashed.

The first three days we fasted I felt hunger pains. Then they too subsided, and I seldom was hungry again. It was almost as if my stomach went to sleep. But I did crave water. In the morning I'd wake up thinking, "I wish Ralph would hurry with that water!" I could hardly wait till he called me. At breakfast we pretended the hot water was coffee or hot milk. At supper we imagined it was tea and different flavors of soup: one day tomato soup, another day beef, then mushroom and chicken, and all the other varieties. Each night when I went to bed I took the vitamin jar filled with boiled water and kept it beside me. When I was wakeful and my mouth felt dry, I sipped the water. Often the water froze in the bottle.

At first we drank water at breakfast, lunch and dinner, three times a day. Then we agreed to skip one "meal," because so much liquid resulted in too much urination. It was too painful a process, baring any part of your body in such cold. From drinking a pint of water a day, we each got down to drinking about a cup: half in the morning, half at "dinner." I trained myself so that, instead of urinating when I first woke up, I could wait until after breakfast, then go once again before I went to sleep at night; later regulating it to once— before I went to sleep.

It occurred to me how curious it is to cling to some silly euphemism of civilization in such circumstances as we were sharing. Each time I took my twice-daily trek, I made some prim comment about "going to the bathroom," if Ralph were nearby—when actually I meant I was going to lean over a fallen log in knee-deep snow and hang onto the branch of a tree for support. In the situation in which we found ourselves, where every bodily function or accident of the flesh was a necessarily shared experience, I was increasingly grateful for Ralph's innate dignity and compassion. I never felt embarrassed around him and, oddly enough, I never felt more feminine in my life than I did during those days with him. Yes, filthy, starving and wounded, I was more conscious of myself as a female than ever before. I don't really know why this should have been; partly perhaps because it was the first time anyone had even taken care of me, as Ralph was doing.

We both were suffering from frostbite in our hands and feet. My right foot remained badly swollen. A large blister had formed around my foot above and beneath the toes. When I took off my canvases and sweaters to examine the blister I found that my toes were black— with the exception of the two middle toes, which were a purplish color. I thought the discoloration was just a bruise. I didn't realize it was the end stage of frostbite. And Ralph didn't tell me. I guess he didn't want me to know my toes were dead.

The blister bothered me, and I asked Ralph to open it with his hunting knife so it would drain. I felt that by draining the blister I could prevent further infection. He didn't want to do it.

"If you won't, I will," I said.

"All right."

He wiped his hunting knife clean with a rag, then held it in the fire a few minutes to sterilize it. Ralph stood over me, knife in hand, looking queasy and hesitant.

I held up my bare foot. "Hurry, it's cold. You've got to do it."

He steadied my foot with his left hand, then, with the knife in his right, made a quick, sharp slice across the top of the blister. It began to drain immediately. I bound the foot in a clean bandage made from one of my cotton dresses, wrapped the sweaters around it, and finally the canvas.

Around the same time when my legs began to ache unbearably from the cold, I asked Ralph to lend me an extra pair of his trousers. But he didn't want to. All my pants were tight-fitting, and I simply could not work another pair over the ones I already had on. Finally, Ralph agreed to let me use an old pair of his. I didn't really mind Ralph's reluctance to contribute his trousers. I just put it down to some odd quirk he had. I'm sure he was making allowances for all my quirks, quirks I wasn't even aware of. And after all, he was, in a very real sense, keeping me alive.

Since Ralph had to keep moving, we treated his feet regularly. I heated water in a can, and helped wash his feet. Then he'd rub them with petroleum jelly as a lubricant. My feet didn't hurt unless I put weight on them. Ralph kept walking constantly, and his feet hurt all the time.

During the second week I got back into the Bible, reading parts of it aloud to Ralph as he worked nearby. I found it more interesting than I had before. It made really good reading. While I read aloud Ralph worked on our two radios, trying to make them really function. Once, during the second week, he actually got one of them going. He strung up some wire on a nearby tree for an antenna and, when a plane passed on the other side of the mountain, started calling. But something suddenly went wrong, and a tube blew out. That was the end of that radio, so Ralph went back to work on the plane's very-high-frequency radio. He seemed to get that one working a little, too, except that the one frequency we really needed—the distress frequency—was broken, and Ralph couldn't fix it.

Still, I kept calling to the passing planes every day they were out, and we did hear them practically every clear day the first two weeks. It was terribly frustrating. They usually came at either eleven in the morning or two-thirty in the afternoon. On bad days they didn't come at all. When the weather was bad, I prayed—for good weather, and for the planes to see us. "Let it be tomorrow!" I prayed. "Let it be tomorrow."

Finally, we decided to give up trying to make contact by radio, and from then on whenever we heard a plane I would limp and lurch, stagger and stumble out of the plane into our little clearing and flash our mirrors through the broken trees up at the sun, hoping someone in a plane would catch sight of the reflecting glare. But no one ever did. If anything, flashing the mirrors was even more frustrating than calling on the radio. Flailing about in the snow, I would get all wet, especially my legs and feet, which would then ache horribly. I remember crying and moaning to myself a couple of times in the cabin where Ralph wouldn't notice me after those mirror-flashing episodes.

Then the planes stopped altogether.

I couldn't believe they'd given up the search.

"Are you sure they know we went down?" I kept asking Ralph over and over.

"Yes," he repeated patiently. "Because we filed a flight plan. When we were overdue in Fort St. John, they must have notified Whitehorse."

"Do you think they can see us here?"

"Yes. When our plane came down, it made a cut in the treetops. Anyone flying over would see that."

Although I knew Ralph was only telling me what I wanted to hear, I still felt somewhat reassured and calm again. And, sure enough, the next clear day, two days later, we heard planes again.

Ralph kept trying to figure out ways to attract them. He decided to make an S.O.S. sign and put it up on the top of a tree where a passing airplane might see it. He managed to tear off a piece of the white-painted aileron from the tail section. Then he found a spray can of yellow paint in the back of the plane. But it was frozen solid, and when Ralph put it by the fire to thaw out, the can exploded all over the place. I remembered I had brought my box of oil paints with me and, rummaging around in the back, I found them. We mixed up a batch of red and put so much linseed oil in the paint it never did dry completely.

We let the sign dry partially overnight, and then Ralph laboriously cut down three spruce saplings, spliced them together with wire, wired the sign to the saplings, then rigged up a rope pulley on a tall tree. But even with the two of us tugging and hauling on the rope together, we couldn't raise that piece of tail section. It was just too heavy for us. So Ralph started all over again —with a smaller piece from the plane. He painted another red S.O.S., let it dry partially, and together we managed to raise it a little above the broken trees.

More than ever I was impressed with Ralph's stamina and perseverance. It seemed to me the biggest difference between us was that Ralph did things while I thought things. He wasn't the least bit curious intellectually, and when I questioned anything he said—such as the divinity of Christ—he didn't like it. He seemed satisfied with his own beliefs without ever questioning them. He was quite ambitious for his family; he had already come a long way in the world from where he'd started in Mexico, and he wanted good things for his children. Remembering my own father, I suspected the best thing he could do for his children when we got out would be to stay home and be a father.

Ralph continued to show a lot of common sense where I was concerned. He was aware, for instance, of my fear of animals. Several times I thought I saw or heard large animals in the brush, and once I heard a frightening cry. But he always talked me out of it, and assured me it was nothing more than owls or one of the rabbits we saw jumping around near the plane. To tell the truth, I wasn't very happy about those rabbits either—especially at night when they came up and scratched and rubbed their backs on the underpart of the plane. It made an eerie sound.

The most frightening noise to me was the roar of the wind up in the tops of the trees. At times it was so powerful it sounded like a fleet of jets screaming down at me. Later I learned to like the wind when it came after a long snowstorm and blew the snow clouds away.

I remember February 18, the fourteenth day after the crash, particularly well, for that was the day Ralph first sang to me. He sang "Happy Birthday" when I mentioned that my birthday was on December 18. We compared notes and later sang "Happy Birthday" to one of Ralph's daughters on February 28, to his wife and my niece on March 1, to my brother Marty on March 4, to my cousin Arthur Gliner on March 5, and to my sister Ruthie on March 6. At first Ralph was shy about his voice, but I told him how much I liked to hear him sing, and he gradually broke down and sang quite a lot during the day while he worked. Ralph knew a lot of songs, Mexican or American. He told me once his idea of a good time was to get four or five men together to play their guitars and sing. We had one long discussion about whether Granada was the name of a city, as I insisted, or a girl, as Ralph said. As usual, Ralph wasn't convinced by my ideas. Since I can't sing a note, I just listened to him. Occasionally I hummed along to keep him company.

One day in the middle of the third week Ralph decided the search planes obviously were unable to see our smoke (that seemed to spread out and drift away among the trees), our mirrors, or our S.O.S. signs, so he decided to make a better signal. He cut some fabric off the side of the plane that had the plane's identification numbers —N5886—on it, and tied this to a long—perhaps twenty-foot—tree he cut down and trimmed. Ralph told me he planned the next day to pull this distress signal by rope up to the top of the tallest tree near us. That tree must have been sixty feet high.

That night I had a wonderful dream, like the ones I used to dream as a kid. Whenever there was anything I wanted to do, and had not yet tried—like skiing, or riding a horse, or skating—I always dreamed about doing it, and practiced it over and over in my dream, so that when I actually did try it, it was somehow familiar. The first time I ever mounted a horse, for example, I simply rode off with no trouble, although secretly I was scared to death of the horse. On this night, though, I dreamed I was the one who put the sign in the top of the tallest tree. After all, who was the greatest tree climber on 78th Street in Brooklyn? I went through the whole process, climbing that great tree, hanging on to the sign. All the while Ralph stood below worrying about me. But I was fine. I got to the very top, anchored the sign so it pointed right up toward heaven, then shinnied back down without so much as a slip or a skinned elbow.

I woke up, exhilarated from my climb; then looked down at my crippled feet. All the excitement drained out of me. I suddenly felt weak, impotent, and for the first time, helpless.

So it was I who stood at the foot of the tree and worried while Ralph made the long ascent. Ralph was a very good climber, but it was a long, long way up, and his fingers and toes were still frostbitten, his ribs and jaw still broken. I not only worried about Ralph; I prayed for him. "God. Please be with him." I prayed he would make it to the top and come back down—without accident. I couldn't face the thought he might fall. If he were injured, I didn't know how he would care for us. For, as the days went by, I was moving less and less. Only in the semicircle near the plane. Even then, I either clung to the plane for support or hung on to tree limbs. I had no control over my feet. If I miscalculated the distance between my supports, I fell. The falls themselves did not hurt me, but the shock of falling unnerved me.

Ralph made it to the top, tied the pole and canvas to the top of the tree with wire and string, and then came back down without trouble. I almost cried with relief.

Still neither of us had too much confidence that a plane would be able to see our new signal, even though it was higher than the other one. Then I had what seemed like a bright idea. "Let's build a forest fire," I suggested. "They're bound to see it."

Ralph agreed to try it.

We picked an area some distance from the wrecked plane, collected a large supply of logs and branches, and set it on fire. But nothing much happened. The fire didn't spread to the surrounding trees. After two hours, it began to die down. A waste of wood. Ralph had already lost interest in my fire, and was trying to make a snare to catch the rabbits that kept hopping about the plane. I tried pulling some logs around, so the flames would draw better. Accidentally, I stepped into the hot coals at the edge, and my foot caught on fire. The flames shot up. This time both the outer canvas and the sweater inside were blazing. I looked from that flaming torch to the nearest snowbank, closed my eyes, and summoned up all my strength, wondering if I could make it. Strength I didn't know I still had flooded through me, and I jumped feet first into the snow. Then I just stood there, quivering from strain and shock, my feet smoking and sizzling slightly as the flames died.

I realized I probably would have burned before calling Ralph. Each time I burned another hole in my canvases or through my hand-socks I felt terribly, stupidly guilty. The one thing Ralph fussed at me about was my carelessness. I still hadn't learned how to adjust to my new awkwardness. I still thought of myself as quick and graceful, and couldn't get it through my head (or feet) that it was no longer true.

That night at supper I knocked over the can of water we were ready to "eat." It was a major catastrophe. We had to start all over again with the oil can of snow. Let it melt, add more snow, melt it, boil it, strain it, reboil it. It was another hour before we had water to drink. He said nothing to me about my stupid clumsiness. Still, it seemed as if everything I'd done that day had gone wrong.

Our biggest problem remained keeping warm at night. We had tried an arrangement with Ralph at the bottom of the sloping floor, me at the top, and our feet together. But it hadn't been comfortable, so we were back where we'd started, lying parallel with our feet toward the center of the plane.

Even though Ralph had hung tarpaulins across the doorway and across the hole where the windshield had been, and even after I had stuffed up every crack I could find with my clothes, it still seemed colder at night inside the plane than out. As we lay against the plane wall, the side next to the metal was always cold, the side nearest Ralph warmer. Because of his broken jaw he slept on his side with his back to me. He couldn't turn toward me. Sometimes when my side was freezing cold I rolled toward him, bent my knees and snuggled against his back.

As I lay there, trying to stay in the same position for an indefinite period of time, thinking all sorts of things, I would try to think thoughts that would induce sleep. Sleep that would blanket the cold, obscure the pain and immobility, and bridge the night. Although deep sleep never came, I welcomed the soft serenity of dozing. I thought of a stanza from Coleridge's "The Rime of the Ancient Mariner" that I had selected to memorize for a class assignment in the ninth grade.

Before the crash, I had often said to myself at night before going to sleep:

> O sleep! it is a gentle thing,
> Beloved from pole to pole!
> To Mary Queen the praise be given!
> She sent the gentle sleep from Heaven
> That slid into my soul.

I don't think Ralph ever slept deeply either. The trick was to lie absolutely still until your own body temperature heated up the air around you. The second you moved you were cold again. But I couldn't stay still. I felt drafts all over. There was a continual ache in my feet, punctuated with sharp, stabbing pains. My legs and knees were always cold, too. And the ruff of my parka would freeze during the night as my warm breath hit it, melt and drip icy water into my face and down my neck all night long. One particular night my feet wouldn't stop throbbing. When I had stayed in one position as long as I could stand it, I began to shift, as slyly as I could, hoping I wouldn't disturb Ralph.

"Leave your feet still," Ralph said.

"But my feet are crying," I said. Then I cried, too.

"Don't cry, Helen."

"I have to," I sobbed.

My mother had sent me a pretty black mohair Italian-knit sweater for my birthday in December, and I kept it under my head at night, pretending it was her breast. I'd been thinking of those nights back home when I'd come in and lie down beside her and tell her what my evening had been like. My mother is a heavy woman, and she always felt very warm, soft, and comforting. Now when I thought of her, it made me cry. I wanted my mother. I wanted to live again.

"Please don't cry, Helen," Ralph said again.

I buried my head in the middle of his parka, across his belly. Ralph didn't pet or baby me but quietly sympathized with me. And I lay there and cried till I was cried out.

VI

Our reactions to hunger were entirely different. While we both dreamed about food practically every night, I didn't really feel too hungry after our food ran out. But poor Ralph was terribly hungry all the time. Like a pregnant woman, I had strange cravings. The first week, I remember, it was for orange juice; later, it was for all kinds of foreign food, particularly Chinese and the Mexican food that Ralph was always talking about—roast chicken and tamales and tacos and enchiladas.

While I had been definitely overweight for several years, my eating habits had always been more psychological than physiological. With no refrigerator to raid, or bowls of goodies to dip into while I read, I really didn't think too much of food. I had actually been a very picky eater, though piggish about anything I really liked. Here with no food visible, no odors of food, no reminders except those we conjured up ourselves, I seldom experienced acute hunger pangs. About the only time I felt my stomach stirring wistfully was when I read sections of the Bible that mentioned the foods of the Middle East: dates and figs and bread and milk and wine and honey. I also thought of halvah, that rich Turkish confection made from ground sesame seeds, and, of all things, knishes, and all the exotic food my mother would buy on the lower East Side.

Perhaps because Ralph worked so much and moved around so much he stayed hungrier than I. Whatever it was, he suffered constantly from gnawing, animal pains that never subsided. Ralph began to look hungrily at the rabbits that jumped in the woods around us. He tied his hunting knife onto a long, pole-shaped spruce limb, and tried to use it as a spear. He would sit for an hour in the evening dusk, waiting, hoping a rabbit would come near enough for him to throw his spear. Once he actually did hit a rabbit with the spear, but the knife just bounced off the rabbit's back, and he ran away. It must have hit his spine.

The next thing Ralph tried was a slingshot he made from the fork of a willow branch, some rubber from one of the plane's wheels and some leather from one of

Distress signal stamped out in snowfield by Ralph Flores.

Cabin of wrecked plane that became Helen Klaben's
and Ralph Flores's first campsite.

Helen Klaben at moment of rescue at second campsite.

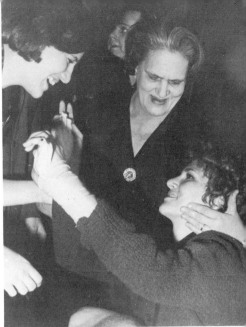

Helen Klaben resting
in rescue plane.

Helen Klaben greeted by mother
and sister Ruth at Idlewild
Airport in New York.

Helen Klaben at Whitehorse
Hospital after rescue

Ralph Flores at Watson Lake,
Yukon Territory Airport, after rescue.

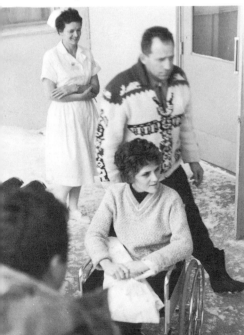

Helen Klaben at Presbyterian Hospital, Harkness Pavilion, in New York City.

the seats. There weren't any little stones around for ammunition, but Ralph dug around in the snow until he found a rock. This he split into little pellets with his hammer, and then fired away with the slingshot. But his stones were all sorts of uneven and asymmetrical shapes, and they flew off in all directions—except in the direction of the rabbit. That was really okay with me because I wasn't too crazy about killing and then eating those rabbits anyway. I wasn't all that hungry.

Then Ralph turned to snares. The first one was made from one of my suitcases—the blue one—and some wire, but as a trap that suitcase made a very good suitcase. After that, his traps became more and more elaborate. He used all sorts of wood and wire and string from the plane, but the one I remember best was a kind of tunnel affair made from spruce branches. It was supposed to have sliding doors and I don't know what all. It was so complicated that I'm sure only a very clever rabbit accustomed to finding his way in mazes would ever have gone into it. And he would have had to have been running full tilt, too. It seemed to me that Ralph never put his traps in the direct line of rabbit traffic, but just sort of anywhere around. I told him he wasn't ever going to catch any rabbits that way, but, of course, Ralph never listened to me. He was probably right. I'm sure I knew nothing about it. So time went by, we looking at the rabbits and the rabbits looking back at us.

I was surprised how little fasting seemed to bother me, and recalled that one of my uncles, who is a health enthusiast, occasionally goes on deliberate fasts for as much as two weeks at a time. If Uncle Jack can do it, I decided, so can I. I asked Ralph how long he thought we could survive with no food.

"Around fifteen days," he said.

That didn't give us very much more time.

Even if we both weren't starving to death yet, we could tell we were getting weaker. Ralph had already used up all the small trees and branches near us and was having to go farther and farther off, and then lug the logs back to the fire. And as the planes kept flying over us, we reluctantly concluded they weren't going to see us. So Ralph decided to build himself some snowshoes that would enable him to get around more easily and let him cover more ground. It took him three or four days to make them out of spruce boughs, cross pieces from some wood from the plane, and wire and string. But even though I told Ralph they were the wrong shape for snowshoes (too long and narrow—like skis), he kept right on, never listening to me. (I'd never made snowshoes, so from his point of view I could see why he didn't pay any attention to what I said.) But when he had the shoes finished, he tried them, and they sank right down into the snow. The next day Ralph started making another pair—this time out of willow wood. He never gave up.

I knew how painful working with his hands must have been for Ralph, for our hands were healing almost identically. The black tissue sloughed off our fingertips, and the new skin underneath was so sensitive it split and cracked from the cold regardless of how we kept our hands bundled up with woolen socks. The socks I was wearing had one hole at about the index finger of my right hand. That became my page-turning finger. When I was reading, I could poke my finger out of the sock, flip the page, then withdraw it hastily into the warmth of the wool before it stung from the cold.

Every so often, I glanced up from the Bible to watch Ralph work. His beard had grown out—thick and black —masking the jagged cuts on his face, his broken jaw and sunken cheekbone. With his heavy beard and steel-rimmed glasses, and my gold fur hat pulled down around his ears, he looked like a soothsayer from a traveling tent show who was down on his luck.

One day I accidentally found a new supply of food. For some reason I brushed my teeth once a week until by mistake I swallowed some toothpaste and commented that it tasted good. Ralph squeezed out an inch or so of the toothpaste, and ate it. I was horrified at first, then gave it a second thought. What could be wrong with toothpaste? It couldn't have anything in it that was harmful, since you were bound to swallow a little each time you used it. I squeezed out a little, put it on my tongue and let it melt slowly. It was almost like food. Sweet in flavor, and with enough substance to make you think you'd eaten. After that, I stopped brushing my teeth, and we ate what was left of my large tube and his small tube. Just a little each day, to make it last and as a precaution against any ill effects. Sometimes we stirred it into our hot water. It tasted delicious. The toothpaste lasted almost two weeks.

On February 25, three weeks to the day after the crash, we heard, then saw a plane. It was a Cessna, and it flew down so low over our little clearing we were sure it had spotted us. We were so excited. We screamed and yelled and danced around, waving and hugging each other, certain we were about to be rescued.

I had somehow lost track of the days and was four days behind on the little calendar I had with me. I thought it was February 21, two days before Ash Wednesday, the first day of Lent, and so I suggested we fast in gratitude. (I had been learning about these things from my reading and discussions with Ralph.) We didn't have our usual breakfast water, and I didn't even eat the last little bit of toothpaste I had left in my tube. We also agreed to fast, if we were rescued, on Ash Wednesday, too—no matter what kind of food we were offered.

The plane did not return. We looked for it all that day. And all the following day. When another day had passed, we realized it was never coming back. Ralph ate a little toothpaste, and I kidded him about breaking his fast. That Cessna was the last plane we saw. We heard a couple of others far away during the next few days . . . and then nothing. Slowly we realized that the air search had been given up. We were really on our own now.

VII

The week after the planes stopped flying over us the bad weather broke, and we began to have some nice, sunny days mixed in with the gray ones. The sun this time of year was never really warm, but there were days when the temperature got up as high as 20 or 30 degrees above zero, and we were able to take off our parkas during the day.

Our days by now had fallen into a fairly set routine. We wakened with daylight, which came around eight o'clock. Since I could look out the window and see a little sky outside, Ralph always asked first thing, "What kind of day is it?"

Usually the sun wasn't up yet. "I can't see yet," I'd say, and we'd wait awhile.

Ralph always said a prayer before he got up. He would sit up and speak aloud. At first, he had prayed, "Please let us go home." Now he added, "If it be Thy will. Please let us go home to our loved ones." Sometimes when he'd pray, I knew he was crying, from the anguish in his voice.

While we waited for the light, I took Ralph's socks and his boots, and sat on them to warm them for him. When they were relatively warm, he wrapped the heavy wool socks and sweaters around his feet, pulled on his galoshes, then crawled out of the plane to start the fire for the day and heat our water.

Often, when the days were warm, Ralph left his parka inside the plane while he cut wood. It took him an hour or more to gather the fire wood, light the fire and heat the water. While he was gone, I'd pull his parka over my own and snooze awhile, feeling more snug and warm during that hour than I had been all night long.

When the fire was going well and the water was boiled and ready to drink, Ralph came back to the plane to wake me, and to help me wrap my feet and climb out of the plane.

"What are we having for breakfast?" I asked.

We'd pretend what we would have that morning: orange juice, bacon and eggs, and milk.

When we had settled down on our log, Ralph said

another prayer. He no longer said grace, as he had when we still had food to eat. Now he thanked God for our strength to carry on, and prayed that He would give our families strength and let them know we were alive. He always ended his prayer with, "In the name of Thine Only Begotten Son, Jesus Christ, Amen." I always joined in the "Amen."

Unless it was a miserable, stormy day, breakfast was generally a delightful time, with the fire burning cheerily and the sun blessing us from above. We had our best conversations in the mornings. We talked about our families and our plans. I told Ralph my mother wanted me to come home and study to become a teacher and then get married and have children. Ralph said he thought that was a good idea; he said it was time for me to settle down, to stop running around without any direction.

Our conversations were always light. I made a conscious effort to entertain Ralph (I felt it was the least I could do). I wanted to be nice to him all the time, so even if I disagreed with something Ralph said, I always tried to keep my tone light and respectful and pleasant.

We talked a lot about marriage. Ralph had some very firm ideas on the subject. He thought the woman's domain was the home, and the man's world was everything outside the house. He did not think the husband should ever criticize his wife about the way she cooked or ran the house, and he could not even consider a wife criticizing her husband about his work or what he

thought about politics or anything like that. I said I
thought marriage was supposed to be sharing and give
and take and exchanging confidences and suggestions
and constructive criticisms and advice and comfort, and
so on and so forth. But Ralph didn't see it that way at
all. And he always ended the conversation by saying I
wasn't married yet, just wait until I got married and
then I'd see. There wasn't much I could say to that.

I wanted to say to Ralph that my marriage couldn't
be that different from our own life together. My husband and I would be able to communicate, and share
interests. I was sure of it. We both realized the harm
it would do if we were to argue, so we compromised. I
humored Ralph, and I imagine he humored me, too. I
guess we both had common sense about it. It grew on
me that common sense is an important part of marriage,
too, as well as love and mutual interests.

Sooner or later, Ralph would start talking about
Mexico and then eventually about his favorite subject:
food. He told me about a Mexican wedding celebration
that would last days or a week, with a "whole roomful
of meat; barbecued whole baby lambs, beef with beans,
tacos, enchiladas . . ." I had never been very adventurous
about food. Now I decided I wanted to taste everything
—including enchiladas. Ralph asked me to come visit
his family in California, and also his relatives and friends
in Mexico. I didn't know what my plans would be after
our rescue, but the idea of visiting Ralph's families in
California and Mexico appealed to me. I had been plan-

ning to go to those places sooner or later, anyway, and, of course, both California and Mexico sounded warmer than where we were.

We talked about Mexico, and then Ralph talked about being Mexican and being discriminated against for being Mexican. He mentioned getting into an argument with a man up on the DEW line and being called a "dirty Mexican" and a "dirty wetback" and a lot of other things. Ralph said he had simply refused to answer the man in defense; he knew he was just as good, that the Mexicans were just as good as anyone else.

I asked Ralph if he were prejudiced against Negroes. He said of course he wasn't. Then I asked him why the Mormon church would not allow Negroes to hold church office. Ralph answered that the Mormons believe the Negroes are descended from Cain and, therefore, God made them inferior and meant them to be punished by having black skin. I told Ralph I simply couldn't believe this, and asked him if he believed it. He said, "That's what it says in the Bible." I said it sounded to me like just another way to rationalize prejudice through the Bible. Ralph didn't like to hear me say things like that, so I changed the subject. Now I've learned that the Mormon church is reviewing its whole position about Negroes. I certainly hope they will be more liberal in their interpretation of the Bible.

I told Ralph several times that Christianity was based on Judaism, and I couldn't understand why he and his fellow Christians didn't know more about the

Jews and their practices. He was still trying to convert me. He said he would like to baptize me himself when we were rescued. He wanted me to testify about our experiences together in his church in California. I didn't want to upset him, so I never said definitely no, just that I wasn't sure what my plans or whereabouts would be after we were rescued.

I was still reading the Bible, sometimes aloud to Ralph, but mostly to myself. During the last week—since the planes gave up searching for us—Ralph developed the conviction we would not be rescued until I finished reading the Bible or accepted Christ or did something he could not quite specify. I, of course, did not share his conviction, but I now felt a powerful compulsion to read the Bible all the way through, to finish it, and to try and understand it. I, too, began to feel there might be some relationship between our being in this predicament and God's plans for me. I tried to think what purpose my death would serve. Perhaps it was something beyond my powers of understanding.

After breakfast, I'd tend the fire for a time while Ralph worked on his second pair of snowshoes. One day he made a kind of sandal for himself out of another piece of airplane tire. He was trying to improve the condition of his feet for walking in snowshoes by keeping his feet exposed in front of the fire. I knew Ralph planned to leave soon, but I didn't want him to. I felt it wasn't necessary to leave, for I was certain we would be rescued wherever we were. But I felt there was less chance if we separated.

As the days went by, I grew weaker and weaker, and moved less and less. I sometimes spent the whole day inside the plane, lying wrapped in the parkas, reading the Bible, or with my head at the door where I could watch Ralph, my face in the sun. When he saw me dozing, Ralph called or came over and woke me. He wanted me to be able to sleep at night. But I was always too cold to sleep well then.

I was usually sorry when he stirred me. For, lying there with the sun on my face, somewhere between sleep and consciousness, I dreamed of delightful things: of lying in the sand at Brighton Beach; and, if I'd just been reading the Bible, of Sabbath and holiday food, and all the fruits I loved—hot mixed fruits and mangoes and avocados. Often I dreamed I was on my way home, my mother and family waiting for me, of all the parties I was planning, of friends, marriage, and lots and lots of people. I missed the exciting whirl and life of New York. "New York's my home," I kept saying over and over. Once I dreamed I went shopping on the lower East Side where they still have their pushcarts and tiny shops, and I bought armloads of fresh fruit from the sidewalk vendors. I dreamed of the theater and ballet, of Fifth Avenue at Christmas.

I wanted to be home for Passover, April 9, when all the family would be gathering together. The house would be warm and bustling and crowded with relatives and children and the children's toys. Everyone would be talking and laughing. It would be wonderful. I dreamed I was home helping my mother prepare the food. In my dream I had a cast on my arm and foot and I was on crutches, but I kept hopping around my mother's kitchen, making *pesadike* cookies.

As I lay there, dreams and daydreams intermingled, myriads of faces swam through my mind: long-forgotten faces of children from grade-school days, adults I had seen on the street or in the subway, but whom I'd never really known. Armies of people marched across my mind's eye. When I asked Ralph about it, he said he saw the same sort of thing. It was as if, isolated from all the human world we had known, we now met in our minds everyone we had ever encountered.

The fifteen days Ralph said we could survive without food came and passed. I knew nothing about record survivals, so I simply settled for the fact we were very much alive and forgot about it. The only thing that worried me was my belly. I kept feeling it and examining it surreptitiously to see if it were changing shape. I thought of the six million Jews who had died of starvation, disease, torture and murder in Hitler's concentration camps, and the pictures I'd seen of the survivors with their skeletal bodies and hollowed-out eyes. I recalled the pictures of tiny Indian and Chinese babies suffering from malnutrition with their grotesquely swollen bellies on matchstick legs. Yet my belly remained flat, my body flesh healthy. There was no distention or hardening or visible bloat. In fact, my skin all over, aside from being dreadfully dirty, was in excellent condition, considering the daily exposure to cold. Under the layer of wood smoke and grime my face was smooth. My nails were long and firm. For the first time in my adult life I didn't bite them. Maybe this was the real secret of a successful diet: just stopping eating altogether.

It amazed me how the weather dictated the way I felt. When I awoke to bright sunshine and a blue sky, I was full of love for God and thanked Him for the beautiful day. At night, as I tried to sleep, I prayed, "Please make it a sunny day tomorrow. Please make the sky blue." On good days when I sat with the sun in my face and a book to read, and I was not too cold or hungry, and I had plenty of water to drink, and Ralph was singing as he worked, I felt content. Then when I had to move I was suddenly miserable.

But if the morning was gray, snowy, cold, and the wind howling high in the trees, I wakened depressed, desolate, forsaken. All I wanted to do was cry. One morning when it was particularly gray and the snow was blowing around us, and my feet ached unmercifully, I began to pray aloud for the first time. I didn't say a specific prayer. I just talked to God, as was my habit, without bothering to preface what I said or say Amen at the end. I just asked him to give strength to my family, since I had been missing for such a long time now.

"God is not listening to you," Ralph said as I finished, "because you did not pray in the name of Jesus Christ."

My emotions gave way, and I fell down onto my parka, sobbing.

"He does too hear me," I screamed at Ralph. "He's heard me for the last twenty-one years. Why do you think He doesn't hear me now?"

I was hysterical and he didn't try to answer, but hastily crawled out of the plane and left me alone. By the time Ralph came back for me an hour later I had control of myself. Neither of us mentioned it again. It was the only time we ever fought—if that was a fight. After that I kept trying to appease Ralph and keep away from controversial subjects. I even got so involved with prayers that once or twice I reminded him to pray when he forgot himself.

That night I was cook. "What do you want for supper?" I asked, as I strained the water.

"Chicken and tacos," Ralph ordered. "Tortillas, tamales . . ."

There were no more planes, but we still occasionally heard the "garbage trucks in Brooklyn"—that faint, intermittent sound in the distance.

"Listen!" Ralph would always call to me. "Keep your ears sharp, Helen. What do you think it is?"

I could hardly catch the distant sound any more. Something had happened to my ears in the past few weeks, and I was having trouble hearing. I wondered if the wax might have frozen inside. I doubted I'd be able to hear a plane, if one ever did fly over again.

I noticed now that we heard no more planes that Ralph paid more and more attention to that distant sound. He would stop whatever he was doing, lift his head and listen with an unnerving intensity. Without his telling me, I knew now he was thinking of trying to find the source of the sound. Was Ralph really going to leave me? I knew he was, but pretended not to notice his preparations, mostly because I wanted him to decide against it by himself.

"It sounds like some sort of engine," Ralph mused. "It could be a mill or saw of some kind. Whatever it is, it's civilization."

"But it's so far away," I said. "It sounds like at least fifty miles."

"Not fifty. Perhaps twenty or thirty."

The next day he tried on his snowshoes. They worked. The way he walked around on them so purposefully indicated to me he had make up his mind to leave. I resigned myself to the fact of his leaving, but tried again.

"God put us here," I said. "He must want us to stay here until we're rescued." I really believed that. I was sure my friend God remembered me.

"There must be people where that sound is," Ralph persisted, ignoring my objections. "Besides"—he looked up at me—"remember the day I climbed that big tree?

I could see a little from up there. There was a river that might lead to the highway if I follow it. Even if I don't reach the sound, I can reach that clearing. It's a better place for an S.O.S. sign than up here in the trees."

As he talked, I realized his mind had been made up for a long time, probably since the planes had stopped searching.

"There's bound to be something not too far from here," Ralph went on. "An Indian camp. A hunting lodge. A highway. Something."

"But what will you do at night?" I asked. "There's no place you can reach in a day, and you'll freeze to death during the night."

"You're going to make me a sleeping bag," Ralph said.

Together we stripped the interior of the plane, pulled the carpet off the floor, the insulation off the walls and ceiling. Then we padded the little pieces of insulation between the carpet and the ceiling cloth.

"I don't know how to sew," I admitted.

"All women sew," Ralph said flatly. "You have a needle and thread."

That was true. My mother had sent me a sewing kit to Fairbanks, and I had used it once—to sew on a button. Now I sat by the fire, the smoke blowing in my face, trying to make a sleeping bag. I never did get it into bag shape. It was far too cumbersome. So I just sewed the sides together, the insulation quilted in the center, and made a big, flat, stuffed blanket.

"Don't you think we better stick together?" I argued to the very last. "It will be the end of us if we get separated." I didn't even mention the possibility of going along with him, and Ralph didn't either. We both knew I couldn't travel without boots—even if I could have stood the pain of walking.

"I know there's something down there, Helen," he said. "We're bound to be near help of some kind. I must go find it."

At last I gave up. "How long will you be gone?" I said.

"From three to six days. I figure even with the deep snow it can't take me more than three days to reach that little lake. I think that engine or whatever it is must be somewhere nearby. Don't worry, Helen. I'll leave you plenty of firewood. And you have water."

"If you can't find the sound, will you come back?"

"Of course I'll come back."

Two days later Ralph left.

In the end, the sleeping bag we'd made was simply too heavy for him to carry, so I took the sleeping bag and gave Ralph my Dynel winter coat with a fake leopard-skin collar. He rolled the coat into a pack, put some matches, his parka, his hammer and chisel, an oil can for snow water and his vitamins inside it, strapped the pack on his back with straps made from the plane's seat belts, and made ready to set out.

I was sitting by the fire with the Bible in my lap. "God be with you," I said softly, and looked up.

In one hand Ralph was holding the airplane's compass, which was quite heavy (perhaps five or six pounds), and in the other the spear he had made. He had a small mirror in one pocket, his binoculars strapped around his neck, and my hat pulled down over his ears.

"Be very careful," I told him. I think I actually felt maternal.

Ralph gave me detailed instructions on what to tell my rescuers, if a plane came in his absence. He seemed afraid I would go off and forget about him. I told him not to forget about me, if he were rescued first.

I just sat on our log by the fire and watched him disappear into the woods. He kept calling back to me so he could judge the distance. "Helen. Hel-enn." First it was loud and close, then it grew fainter until it was no more than an echo in the forest. But I continued to sit there on our log, calling his name at regular intervals long after I could no longer hear my own.

VIII

The day after Ralph left, the temperature dropped, the wind started howling through the trees, and there were snow flurries. I worried about Ralph. He had only his parka and my coat for cover and warmth. I was afraid he would freeze to death.

My legs were terribly cold. I decided to borrow another pair of Ralph's trousers. They were in one of his trunks that he had taken outside the plane and placed against the fuselage. To my surprise and bewilderment, I found the trunk locked. Ralph must have locked it just before leaving. His other trunk—the one with all his religious books—he had left unlocked. I brooded for a while about this strange quirk of Ralph's and then decided to forget about it, since there wasn't anything I could do about it anyway.

That was one of the few times I ventured outside the plane for the next week. I realized that because of the bad weather no planes would be likely to stray over me or my signal fire. Before he'd left, Ralph had always been the one to make the fires. He had taught me how to do it the last few days. Although Ralph had said he was going to leave me plenty of wood, in the end he cut up only enough for what I calculated might last three days —the minimum time he'd said he would be gone. There was also a pile of green pine for smoke signals in case I ever did hear a plane. I don't know what I did wrong, but I couldn't make the fire work well. Some of the wood burned nicely, but most of it seemed to smoke a lot, and smell. If I got close enough to get warm, the smoke blew in my eyes and the fumes made me cough.

So I stayed inside most of the time. It did not take me long to realize I was warmer than when Ralph had been with me. The crude sleeping blanket I had made from the plane's insulation and carpeting was very snug. If only we had thought of it before, we would have saved ourselves from all those miserable nights.

I think the worst thing about my being alone was time. My watch had been broken in the crash. Ralph had let me wear his self-winding wrist watch occasionally when we were together, but I wore it on my broken arm and didn't move it enough to keep it wound. Naturally, Ralph took his watch with him when he left. He gave me the clock from the plane, which had also broken in the crash, but which he had repaired. The clock stopped the day after Ralph left. I tried to make it run by shaking it and standing it on its head, but it never gave even one encouraging tick. It was dead.

So I had no way of telling time. That first day was cloudy, and it was impossible for me to tell if it was 2 P.M., 4 P.M. or 5 P.M. Should I try to sleep now? I wondered. Or should I read a few more hours? It was like living in the Twilight Zone. Just the gray, timeless nothingness.

The next day it snowed. So long as the snowstorm kept up it was a gray-white world, without hours or sunlight. Thoreau wrote that he found it charming to be without time. I didn't. Sometimes in New York, when I resented the tempo that dictated my life, or rather the tempo *I*, myself, dictated, I would stop wearing a watch in rebellion—against the "system" and myself. But now time was my only tie to civilization or, anyway, one of its last symbols. And I had lost it.

That started me thinking about what civilization was really like, now that I was no longer in it. I realized that a lot of things I had always just taken for granted— like a bed to sleep in, hot water and soap, three meals a day, my phonograph or radio and television or movies, or just someone to talk to—were more like luxuries, not the necessities I had assumed. These things just weren't as important as I had thought.

Now that I was alone I realized the advantage of getting lost with a man like Ralph was not only the assurance of someone there to protect me if anything happened, but also the opportunity to spend time by myself to think and reflect. For instance, if some animal would try to come up and bite me, I knew Ralph would shoo it away. Now that he was gone I had to face my fears. I hoped the animals in these woods would be as friendly as those in *Snow White*. I kept the tarpaulin over the door and hardly looked out the window on the assumption that what I didn't know or see wouldn't hurt me. I was going to die; I wasn't afraid of being alone. For the first time in my life I was *really* alone and, to my surprise, I found it wasn't so bad.

March 8, the day after Ralph left, one month and four days after we'd crashed, I started to keep a sort of diary—in the form of a letter to my family.

"To all my loved ones, especially my dearest, most wonderful mother:

"It's been over a month since I left Fairbanks—or civilization," I began. "I am sitting in the plane somewhere in the Yukon or perhaps British Columbia writing this testimonial. I waited this long hoping to be able to write it at home. Now I'm sorry I didn't write this adventure as a daily log.

"There is so much I want to say. So much we've learned. My foremost desire is to be home with you now.

And with the mercy of our most generous Lord I will be soon, I pray."

I went on for a page or so, describing my decision to make the trip, my meeting with Ralph, our time together in Whitehorse at the Taku Hotel, finally taking off. . . . But when I came to the crash, I couldn't go any further. The whole thing sounded too much like an epitaph, and I quit. There's no point writing the end, I told myself, till the end has come.

The next day there was a real blizzard. I got out Robert Service and read about his blizzards and compared them. This one wasn't quite as terrible as the ones he described, but it was bad enough. There was one passage in a poem called "The Parson's Son" that seemed so close to my own situation that I kept returning to it over and over.

> Look at my eyes—been snow-blind twice;
> Look where my foot's half gone;
> And that gruesome scar on my left cheek where
> the frost-fiend bit to the bone . . .

Although I felt quite shaken up by the words, I realized I wasn't in as bad a condition as the man in the poem.

The last stanza of "The Law of the Yukon" also seemed to me terribly apt.

> This is the Law of the Yukon, that only the Strong shall thrive;
> That surely the Weak shall perish, and only the Fit survive.

Dissolute, damned and despairful, crippled and palsied
    and slain,
This is the Will of the Yukon,—Lo, how she makes it
    plain!

I stayed burrowed in the blanket, hoping Ralph had
found some way to protect himself.

So long as it snowed I knew no planes would come
over. I decided to let the fire go out and just stay inside
the plane, covered up in the blanket, and read away the
time. I boiled enough water to last a few days—but it
froze. I also put one of the oil cans at hand to use as a
urinal. Then I settled into my insulated blanket, with
my books at hand, my conveniences close by, to wait out
the storm—and Ralph's return.

By now the bandage on my arm had gotten un-
raveled, and I had always felt it was too tight, anyway, so
I undid the whole thing. My arm, when I had it un-
wrapped, looked so white and skinny and yet swollen
from the tight wrapping. I put the splints back on and
rebound it loosely so my arm could breathe. It felt
better.

Since I had privacy, I examined my body more
closely. I hadn't known I had cuts on my legs until they
began to itch a week after we crashed. Now they all
seemed to be healing nicely, with only a few half-moon
scars on my leg and knee and ankle. I unbandaged my
feet and bathed them. They always hurt more after they
had been bathed, but I felt they should be kept as clean

as possible. The blisters on my heel were more or less
the same, but the lower section of my right foot seemed
to have worsened. Underneath the black crust the flesh
seemed to be disintegrating. I could see the outline of
the bones. My foot smelled as if it were rotting away, so
I quickly wrapped it up again. I suppose I should have
been scared, but I wasn't.

It was a trial to know what to do with my feet now.
When I put them down they throbbed. Yet it was difficult to keep them up, particularly in the plane, where
the angle was awkward. I still thought my foot and toes
were alive because of the intensity of the stabbing pains,
which I assumed was blood circulating. I kept imagining
what would happen when I was rescued, and I always
visualized my foot in a whirlpool bath.

My dirty condition was bothering me by now, too.
My hair was grimy and smelled and my scalp itched all
the time, especially at night when I was chilled and restless. When I couldn't stand it any longer, I'd finally get
one hand out from under the covers and slip it under
my hood and scratch.

Yet your body at a time like that becomes curiously
removed from yourself. It is an outer thing you care for
and contemplate objectively. Things have happened to
it and are happening to it, but it's almost as though your
body belonged to someone else. The worse the things
that happen to your body the more you tend to withdraw
into yourself. Eventually you feel like an small inner
core surrounded by a physical problem that you cope

with as best you can. After a while, it doesn't even concern you very much. You are you: the creature inside,
busy with your thoughts and dreams. When the body in-
trudes, you treat it as a kindly nurse would, then go
back to your own inner self again.

I looked through my Great Books, remembering the
first book "without pictures" I had ever read. It was a
Nancy Drew mystery. Linda Goldstein lent it to me
when I was sick. I had let it sit around the house for a
while, and then when I finally did start I became a
Nancy Drew addict. I didn't quit till I finished the book.
Then I read all the other Nancy Drews.

Now I tried the Communist Manifesto. "The history of all hitherto existing society is the history of class
struggles." But I couldn't concentrate properly and put
it down after only three chapters, and picked up the
Bible again. Although I had been reading the Bible
fairly regularly before Ralph left, I now felt a powerful
compulsion to get completely through it, to read it from
beginning to end, even if I did not actually read all the
chapters in consecutive order.

I had started with the Old Testament, most of
which I was at least familiar with, although I had never
actually sat down and studied it. The Book of Job held
me particularly. I related everything I read to myself and
the position I was in, and it was easy to compare my
trials to Job's. I prayed God would reveal Himself to
me, that He would be with me, fill me with His love,
fulfill and protect me.

From Job I began to jump around, reading at random. I read through the Gospel according to St. Matthew again, then went back to the Old Testament. Next I skipped up to the Gospel according to St. Luke. Then I went back and finished up the Old Testament— except for the Psalms and Proverbs, which I saved to nibble at between the long narrative books. I read the Epistles, then went back and completed the Gospels according to Mark and John. And then I came across the Ten Commandments.

The Ten Commandments are pretty much the same in both the Protestant and Jewish Bibles, although the numbering and some of the wording differ. I read them slowly, testing my own actions against each one, looking back on my life, reflecting on what I had done.

Thou shalt have no other Gods before me. Everyone has his own concept of God. If God is synonymous with goodness, though, then everyone worships the same God and God is, therefore, One, no matter what rules of worship we abide by.

For me, the most important rule of human behavior is simply and beautifully stated: Love thy neighbor as thyself, and do unto thy neighbor as thou wouldst have done unto thee. That, I feel, is the basis of goodness and love. And the commandments, although great and compelling in themselves, are still only subcategories of this rule.

Remember the Sabbath Day, to keep it holy. This is necessary, it seems to me, in the same way formal prayer is necessary. Both are easy to forget. The observance of the Sabbath keeps us cognizant of our laws of life, of God and goodness and of ourselves.

The Bible, it occurred to me then, is inspiring because it makes us realize the many hurts we inflict upon each other unknowingly. It can be read as a guide to exercising good character control. It can also be read as a great comforter and healer, because not only does the Bible make us realize all we have to be grateful for, it also shows us that, whatever our suffering, much greater suffering has been lived through before by others.

The Bible seemed to say to me that keeping God in our hearts encourages an inner tranquillity and peace of mind.

Blessed *are* they which do hunger and thirst
after righteousness: for they shall be filled.

And from Jonah a passage that seemed especially moving and meaningful to me:

...I cried by reason of mine affliction unto the Lord,
and he heard me;
out of the belly of hell cried I,
and thou heardest my voice.
For thou hadst cast me into the deep...

When my soul fainted within me I remembered the
    Lord;
and my prayer came in unto thee,
into thine holy temple...

They that observe lying vanities forsake their own mercy.
But I will sacrifice unto thee with the voice of thanks-
     giving;
I will pay *that* that I have vowed.
Salvation *is* of the Lord.

Being true to yourself, I realized, is the most important step in accepting yourself. I began to realize my own
limitations in reading the Bible, and I was sure not to
make any vows without thinking it over a few days just
to be certain I thought I would be able to keep them. It
would be useless to burden myself with self-inflicted
guilt pangs for not being able to keep vows I had no
business making in the first place.

While reading the Bible, of course, I applied everything to myself as a yardstick. I admit I certainly didn't
measure up to all the Bible's expectations or even my
own. I did feel, however, that a lot of the tenets did not
apply to me, but perhaps I was merely rationalizing away
those I felt were too hard. In order to be godlike, according to Moses and Jesus, I would have to renovate my
personality. I knew I couldn't go all the way, but I intended to change my ways in certain areas.

Honor thy father and thy mother. This command-
ment brought so many thoughts to me—both happy and
unhappy. It's strange. My mother never pushed religion
at her children, nor did she exercise any rules or regula-
tions or special discipline or even supervision. More-
over, she never displayed much outward show of affec-

tion for her children. With this kind of upbringing it would be natural to expect all sorts of juvenile delinquency. Yet not one of my brothers or sisters was ever involved in anything like that. We all turned out the better for our lack of discipline and supervision.

The more I thought about my family, the more I realized I was very proud of them. Martin is still going to night school for a degree in electrical engineering. Eddie owns a large camera store. Robby is an accountant. Ruthie is a bookkeeper. Arthur is a chemical engineer. Linda is a junior stock analyst and is taking courses at a school of finance.

As I waited all alone for Ralph to come back, I realized I was never able to appreciate my family until I was away from them. Despite all the familial fights and antagonisms and teasing, I was always able to rely upon any one of them in a time of crisis. We would all stand together. I was so proud of them. The Bible says not to be proud, but I couldn't help it. I didn't feel it was bad.

Sitting huddled under my blanket in the freezing airplane, with the Bible in my hands and my family in my heart, I started thinking again of the journey I had made that took me away from all of them, of driving across the country with Sue Beehler, of arriving in Fairbanks, and of everything that happened to me there that changed my life and changed me....

IX

Everyone, it seemed, was going to Europe. But I wanted to see America first. Just so that if anyone in Europe would ask me about America, as I would ask about Europe, I would have firsthand knowledge, and make more interesting conversation. Besides, since it would be my first trip away from home, my mother would feel better about me, not having an ocean between us, even though the distance in mileage would be about the same.

Traveling alone seemed out of the question to everyone else but me. They tried to persuade me with facts about expense, loneliness and safety for a girl all by herself. Although my friends were willing to talk about how exciting it would be and the adventure of it, when it came down to action, no one was ever there. They said it cost too much or they couldn't afford the time. I've met so many planners in my life it's disgusting. From these people I've learned to keep my mouth closed until I am ready to do something. There's nothing so boring as having to listen to someone's futile plans.

In New York, one of my little ambitions was to be the stereotype of the young sophisticate, not even knowing what it was. But it seemed very stimulating—the world of intellectuals and knowledgeables. I realized I didn't have anything to offer in the way of smart talk, anecdotes, gossip, beauty, fame or even experience. The best way to gain experience, I decided, was to Expose Myself to Life.

It seemed I was leading the life of a robot—the lament of almost everyone who works in a New York office. Wake up, decide what to wear, travel an hour to work, work eight hours, another hour traveling home, and, in my case, to school, dinner, unwind, then to sleep. The same ritual the next day and the day after and the day after. . . . No matter what interesting diversions I would involve myself in, everything was the same.

It was not as though I wasn't trying. I had a challenging job; I was enrolled in Advanced Special Study at Pratt Institute, taking abstract painting, metal sculpture, photography and other courses; I was a member of the Museum of Modern Art and spent much of my little free time there; I was doing a lot of ice skating in Central Park and taking ballet lessons. . . . Yet, I couldn't find myself in anything. Everything came too easily and meant too little.

I thought perhaps the missing link in my life was sex. You certainly hear a lot about it in what I took to be sophisticated circles: So-and-so is running around with So-and-so; her boss has wild parties instead of going home; boy! has So-and-so a lot of dates and you know why! Sex turns the world. Everyone does it. Et cetera, et cetera, et cetera.

Well, I decided to travel. In the *New York Times* personal-advertising column a girl wanted a traveling companion to go to Los Angeles. I really wanted to go to San Francisco, but thought Los Angeles sounded just as good. By an odd coincidence, the girl happened to live nearby. She seemed to like me, but was at first dubious about me, for some reason. When I told her I was Jewish, however, she became suddenly much warmer because she was Jewish herself and decided to take me along instead of any of the other girls who had responded to her ad. In a way, that sort of amused me. Apparently I don't look or sound particularly Jewish, although occasionally I use what are considered Jewish inflections in my speech. It's fun every once in a while to talk that way.

Anyway, we made all sorts of plans. My mother met her mother. Her family met and approved of me. But the girl kept putting off our departure date because, first, her mother was sick, and then for all sorts of other reasons. In the end, the girl had too much luggage to pack in the back of the car—I think she was taking at least six winter coats to Southern California, of all places. So the girl decided to fly to California instead.

I was very disappointed. I had been ready to leave for the past week. Now what? Perhaps there would be another ad in the *Times* for a passenger to California. If I have to wait another two weeks, I told myself, I'll end up screaming. Sure enough, though no one in the *Times* was going to California that Tuesday morning, there was a girl going to Alaska.

My mother continued to have mixed emotions about my leaving home. Alaska was even farther away than California. She never outwardly expressed fear for my welfare. She suggested several reasons for my not going: my responsibility to the family, my reputation, my future. At the same time, she realized the importance of Experience for me. She knew I would not be happy if I married before I satisfied my curiosity about the rest of the world. My mother has had a hard life, but she has never burdened her children with details, and only confided in me when I pressed her to. She never talks about her hardships during childhood, or rather her lack of childhood.

Though she worried, I think my mother saw in me the chance she never had to explore the world. She talked with curiosity about Alaska. It sounded to both of us as remote as Africa and just as intriguing. I couldn't imagine how people lived on ice in below-zero temperatures. In igloos, like Eskimos, maybe. How-to-trap-a-man advisors in magazines and newspapers were always suggesting Alaska as a last resort because there weren't any women up there, but as far as I was concerned hunting season was not yet open. Nor was I going all the way to Alaska to do something I didn't want my mother to know about.

The prime reason for my going to Alaska is easily stated. I knew I didn't know anything about Life, and I thought perhaps I would feel less lonely, less unhappy, less aimless, less unsatisfied if I exposed myself to new experiences and to new people. I also felt very keenly that I could never be truly happy until I learned to give something of myself, until I learned to love someone or something, and learned to receive love in return. This wasn't happening to me in New York. Consciously, as well as subconsciously, I must have hoped something like that would occur to me. Alaska was just one destination in my life of many I hoped to reach—and still hope to reach.

Sue Beehler had traveled extensively throughout the United States, and had just returned from a trip abroad. She seemed to know what she was doing, and I had a lot of confidence in her. We decided to leave on the coming Friday—August 25, 1962. To switch from destination Los Angeles to destination Alaska, I had to unpack, dig up my winter clothes on a terrifically hot summer day, and repack, trying to squeeze everything in. Sue suggested we take some camping gear in order to save money on the trip across the continent (I had $700 saved and took $400 of it with me). I had never slept in a sleeping bag before, although I had been on an over-night camp-out one summer. But I hadn't slept.

We somehow managed to pile everything on top of Sue's Volkswagen. My mother smiled very bravely, and I was so grateful to her for that. I just couldn't believe I was on my way at last. Me, Helen, leaving Brooklyn. Driving all the way to Alaska. I had just gotten my driving license, but I didn't know how to drive a standard-shift car, much less a V.W., although I had taken two lessons the day before. Sensing my inexperience, Sue did not let me drive until we got out into open country—in Minnesota.

I repeatedly thought how great it was to be an American. How beautiful, how varied, how free. I thought of myself crossing the country as one of the pioneers might have in a covered wagon. It is really fantastic to think of people making their way through virgin country. No highways, no turnpikes, no bridges, no Howard Johnsons, no Volkswagens. I tried to im-agine how it would feel to be the first one in the whole world to see the plush, fertile land beyond the Appalach-ians, to travel for the first time across the seemingly endless plains of the Middle West. I imagined I could see the Indians lined up for an attack on the edge of the

buttes, not even bothering to wait to massacre us in the
gullies in the mountainous West.

To me, the cows were just as fascinating as the
usual tourist attractions: Niagara Falls, Marshall Field's
and the Loop in Chicago, Frank Lloyd Wright's Taliesin
and the House on the Rock in Madison, Wisconsin,
Mount Rushmore, Yellowstone National Park, the
World's Fair in Seattle. Most of all, though, the people
impressed me, their openness, their friendliness. Those
that I met in restaurants, gas stations, motels weren't
hicks, as I had thought anyone outside New York to be.

We met no robbers, sex maniacs, murderers or con
men, as we had been assured was practically inevitable.
The only mishaps in the entire four thousand miles were
one flat tire that occurred just outside a gas station, and
a second on a muddy shoulder of the Alaska Highway. I
thought it very exciting because I had never had to
change a tire before, but we weren't even able to un-
screw the nuts before some men stopped and finished
the job for us. The car also sustained a cracked battery
from one of the numerous rocks that seemed to jump
up from nowhere on that rough road. We were left
sitting in a car reeking with battery acid. Everyone was
very kind and interested in giving us a push to get
started. We were unable to get a new battery for the next
days until we reached Whitehorse. A man who had
been following behind us on the highway for the last few
days was familiar with Whitehorse, and gave us a grand

tour of the town. He showed us the landmarks of the Gold Rush days, and Sam McGee's house, and recited the poem by heart. (Later, I tried to recite it for Ralph.)

> There are strange things done in the midnight sun
> By the men who moil for gold;
> The Arctic trails have their secret tales
> That would make your blood run cold;
> The Northern Lights have seen queer sights,
> But the queerest they ever did see
> Was that night on the marge of Lake Lebarge
> I cremated Sam McGee . . .

The closer we got to Fairbanks, where Sue's cousin Marcia and her husband Ray Hoffman, an Air Force dentist, were stationed, the more excited we became. Neither of us knew very much about Alaska, or Fairbanks, in which we arrived after seventeen days. The impressions we had were of a very prosperous city and, at the same time, a frontier town where someone with drive and ambition could make a fortune at anything he had in mind. We thought we would homestead some land near town, planning the buildings and the crop rotation. I thought I might like to build a lodge similar to the Old Faithful Inn in Yellowstone National Park. It would be an intimate haven for hunters, fishermen and skiers.

My first disillusionment came when I found I could not become a teacher; not that I really wanted to teach, but I thought it would have been a good job to take before making up my mind what I did want to do. I was under the impression that anyone with any college background would be qualified. I was wrong. A couple of months previously, legislation had been passed to raise the standards of education, and now only college graduates were acceptable.

Sue remained living on the Air Force base with her cousins and taught there, and we soon lost contact with each other. I checked into a roominghouse—"Vi's Smorgasbord." The rooms were rented predominantly to men. I was the only girl. Rather than engage a tiny room with a bathroom in the hall for $20 a week, I took the one big room that had a private bath and a refrigerator for $30 a week. The room actually accommodated about five people, but I preferred it to getting claustrophobia in a smaller room. I had never lived in an apartment before.

Now I *was* all alone, four thousand miles from home. I didn't know a soul except for Sue and the Hoffmans, who were twenty-six miles from town. I had no phone. I didn't have a job. I had only $200 of the $400 I had taken with me. I wanted to make it on my own, without sending home for money, even though I had left $300 with my mother for that purpose. I was secure, knowing that if I ever really needed anything I could always count on my family. Nevertheless, I was on my own for the first time in my life. Really alone. The first nights were strange in my new home, for the apartment house was next door to a kennel full of Alaskan Huskies. They howled early in the morning and late at night.

The first day I set out looking for a job with all the confidence of a "sophisticated" New Yorker. I could teach those know-nothing non-New Yorkers something, and everyone would see my talents. I hit the town in my all-black Madison Avenue attire, with my hair styled by Enrico Caruso (before I left New York) in the Marienbad style. I felt terribly chic. The movie and the hair style had obviously not yet reached Fairbanks. I found out later at the single movie theater in town that the films were usually from six months to ten years old.

The first thing I did was to sign up with the State Employment Agency. I wanted a very interesting, diversified job, with a very good salary, I told them. Perhaps in an Eskimo village. A job that would enable me to travel and also save money. Of course I realize there aren't many jobs like that anywhere in the world; I didn't find one like it in Fairbanks. But I didn't want just a clerical job. I hadn't come four thousand miles for that.

I finally accepted—out of both interest and financial necessity—a job in a photographic studio. I had become very interested in photography recently, and thought I might be trained as a photographer or work in a darkroom, since I had had some experience at Pratt Institute. My job, in fact, was soliciting business by telephone. Since the people at the other end of the phone were never particularly enthusiastic about being approached in this manner, I never felt a sense of accomplishment even when I did interest some gullible soul in having a picture taken. Besides, I seemed always to be waking people from sleep. I felt bored and misplaced and unappreciated, so I quit.

Back on the street again, I enjoyed people-watching—and there were so many interesting people to watch on Second Avenue in Fairbanks. Real live Eskimos. And men—I never saw so many men! All looking at me. There were lots of souvenir shops and bars. Some bars were cocktail lounges, others were soldier hangouts, and others were for Eskimos only. Eskimos are as discriminated against in Alaska as are Mexicans in California and Negroes in the South.

Everyone I met was very friendly and willing to help a damsel in distress. I was referred to lots of possibilities for employment; so many that I soon knew Fairbanks as well as Manhattan and developed a sense of belonging to the town. Side by side were modern apartment houses and log cabins from the frontier days. Fairbanks is still such a new town that its history is still fresh and alive everywhere about you on all the streetcorners and even in many of the natives.

One of the first "real" people I met in Alaska was Fred Pankratz. I was in the Weins Airline office, asking about a job as a stewardess, because I thought that might be a good way to see the Northwest country, and Fred just stood at the counter, unabashedly listening while I talked to the girl behind the counter. She told me to take a taxi out to the Fairbanks airport and speak to the personnel manager at their field office. Later I bumped into Fred in the street, and he told me not to let them send me on a wild goose chase. "I know they aren't hiring stewardesses right now, and there's no sense in your wasting your time or money."

I was surprised at his concern. He spoke firmly and directly, and I felt he must know what he was talking about. Alaskans' friendliness had already amused me. By nature generally friendly myself, I was still accustomed to the eyes-ahead attitude of big-city dwellers. Here everyone spoke with a lack of formality that made me feel easy and delightfully casual. Alaskans had a very natural and sincere type of hospitality. I later found out that no one thought I was sleek and sophisticated, as I supposed, but rather a green, naïve kid.

Over a cup of coffee, Fred Pankratz and I started to get to know each other. The more I found out about Fred and his life the more it seemed to me he represented everything I like about Alaska—the open, frontier quality, the diversity, strength, versatility and ruggedness. At that time, Alaska was, I gathered, riptooting, wide-open, shotgun-law territory. Whenever Fred and his friends gathered, I would live vicariously the fantastic tales of the North.

When I met Fred he was finishing off a construction season and starting once again plans for the development of one of his numerous mineral claims. Nome Gold Coast, of which he is both president and promoter, represents extensive gold claims off the coast of Nome. Apparently, some of the local town leaders oppose proposed tax incentives to encourage speculation and prospecting, and Fred, in an effort to promote the development of these claims and the area, travels to New York, Mexico, California, Hong Kong and, of course, all over Alaska.

About the time I first met Fred, he and his colleagues of Nome Gold Coast were preparing a prospectus. He allowed me to do some research at the University of Alaska, and I involved myself for a time in this very interesting work.

Through a friend of Fred's I learned there was a need for draftsmen at the Bureau of Land Management. I didn't know what a draftsman did exactly, but with my art background I thought I would be able to cope with it, and from previous experience I knew I was able to learn very quickly without revealing my ignorance. I remembered the time I got my initial experience with a Leroy Lettering Set, which is a necessary tool for drafting and is easy to learn to use, but takes practice before one is proficient with it. I was working at the Mel Richman Art Studio in New York during the final days of its existence. During this time, I met an anatomy professor from New York University, who was writing a text book that required many charts and graphs. He asked me if I would like to do them, and I, not even knowing then what a Leroy Lettering Set was, said I would. Back at work, the office manager taught me how to use the instruments and advised me on layout. With lots and lots of practice, I finally did the job.

I had expected drafting to be terribly dull, but there was some short-lived excitement at the beginning. I got esthetic pleasure from the sharp black lines on the white paper. There was a challenge in plotting bearings. I also received an unexpected education in geography and federal land law versus state land law.

I was not used to bureaucratic form of employment, and as hard as I tried I was not able to adapt my thinking to accepting the chain of command and rating slots and all the rest of it. I sort of placidly rebelled against what I regarded as authoritarianism. I can't say my placid rebellion was the cause of my perpetual lateness to work, because I have always arrived late and it is just a chronically bad personality trait that I am still trying to overcome. But aside from my lateness, my boss, Pete Reader, told me he thought I did very good work.

I think some excerpts from a letter I wrote home in October show what my job and life were like at that time.

Dear Family,

Again, today is Sunday and another week has gone by—I have been here for more than a month. At this time I am nostalgic. What would I be doing now if I were home? How has this move ultimately changed my life? I am in the heart of Alaska—truly God's country. Winter is here. It has snowed all weekend, with no sign of warmer temperatures. Last night it fell to 15 degrees. I was unaware of this, even though I had only two sweaters on. Guess my blood is getting thicker. My initiation cold is gone—after traveling around my head for the last three weeks. I am familiar with the street names and know where things are—not everything yet; I'm still learning. My reaction to this town is similar to getting acquainted with an unknown relative.

I am having a grand time at work. There are 5 draftsmen and we are all in one room. The immediate boss is not there. We are all young. There are two boys —one, Dave, nineteen, the other, Roger, twenty-two, and both are at a stage when all they think about is sex. Roberta is a bit older—the other, Elaine, and I are quite friendly (have our coffee breaks together). We are always talking. I never talked so much in my life. Elaine is a farm girl at heart and is homesick for Montana. Roberta is from Virginia and speaks with a Southern drawl. The boys have lived up here for a long time with their parents. . . .

A new girl moved in here. Sylvia—she is twenty-one. She is another big-city girl—from Chicago. Just as I did, she came here on a lark. We have lots in common (she is a Sagittarian, too). And she is single—hardly any single girls up here, other than Eskimos and high-schoolers. As a nurse, she works odd shifts at the hospital.

Anyway, last night we went roller skating. The crowd was made up of local kids and GI's—the twenty- and twenty-one-year-old variety. The ratio was about ten boys to each girl. I was never more popular. . . . I wasn't able to skate a full lap with one boy. It got pretty disgusting after a while. I wouldn't have minded if they were older. . . . But nevertheless I had a real fun time skating. . . .

This afternoon I went to a concert of a violinist and pianist—it was very good. I am trying to take advantage of the limited cultural activities, of which this was the monthly concert series . . .

It is now Monday night and I am writing this during a break in my geology course; which is kinda dull. . . .

Heard President Kennedy's report to the nation [about Cuba]. What is N.Y.'s reaction? Here is mixed emotions. My office at work has been carrying on frantically—planning on bomb shelters, etc. . . .

In the same letter, I also wrote just to my sister Linda, telling her how much I missed her and how interested I was in what she was doing.

After a while, I decided to move closer to town into a place with a full kitchen. The building was a two-story efficiency apartment house that reminded me of a houseboat. It was across the Cushman Street Bridge on the bank of the Chena River. My apartment was a small, modern affair. I liked it, but could never get used to its compactness. My boss, Pete Reader, lived across the hall. I was able to hear the man in the next apartment snore in the quiet of the night.

The place was one of the nicest in town. And it was

here that I felt completely domesticated. I did all my own laundry in a wringer-type washing machine, and my own cleaning. I was immaculate when I wasn't a slob. And I did my own shopping and cooking. It wasn't as if I had never done these things before; it was just that now if I didn't do them no one else would, and I would be the only one to suffer the consequences. Complete freedom perhaps, but never really free from oneself.

I met Ernette in the laundry room of the house. She taught me to operate the washing machine and gave me innumerable tips on housekeeping. She was my age and single also—from a small town in Pennsylvania. We became very friendly and spent lots of late nights comparing notes. She is another added to my list of friends who met her husband while I was with them. I convinced her that going into one of the better bars unescorted in Fairbanks was socially acceptable, although it's not (to me, anyway) in New York. It is like a soda fountain, where one would go to meet friends and dance. I like dancing—especially the twist. It's good exercise.

In November, winter really set in. The Geological Institute predicted 80 below zero, and I kept watching daily to see what that phenomenal figure would feel like. It never did get there. Our record for the winter was 53 below. Some mornings it was so cold that the automobile tires had frozen solid overnight. They would jolt and bounce the cars around until the friction thawed them out again. One day I was told it was so cold that if

I threw a pan of hot water up in the air it would freeze on the way down and form snowflakes. I filled a pan of water, leaned out the window so I could see what would happen, and heaved. I got soaked.

The worst part of the winter was not the cold but the loss of light. There were less and less hours of daylight until by December we had no more than two hours each day. It seemed strange to go to one of the supermarkets, trudging through the dark, subzero streets, and find the same scene as in Brooklyn: the same aisles of canned goods, gleaming fluorescent lights overhead, women, occasionally accompanied by their husbands, loading the same wire shopping carts. It was only when they bundled up and went out into the dark street that they became distinguishably Alaskans. And it was only when you looked at the prices on the shelves that you realized you were in Fairbanks and not Brooklyn.

The darker it got the more active I became. I got outfitted in Alaskan gear—boots, parka, sweatshirt with a hood, thermal underwear; I went caribou hunting (didn't get one); took a flight in a small plane; panned for gold; skied and ice-skated; joined the University of Alaska Drama Club; enrolled in the Great Books course; took up painting again; bowled on a team every Friday night; and in addition to the geology course I also took one in fencing at the U.S.O. with my friend Sylvia.

I went out all the time. While at home it was customary to have a gang of girl friends and be on the lookout for a boy, in Fairbanks it was the reverse. As a single girl, you automatically had a herd of men to choose from, but had to shop for girl friends. In Alaska, there aren't many Jews (or girls from Brooklyn, for that matter), and often I was the only Jew in a group. I soon realized that a lot of people didn't know I was Jewish, but I found that when anyone asked about my religion I always said, "I'm a Jew." It was more important to me than I had realized.

Being Jewish makes less difference in Fairbanks than it does in New York. People there are all wanderers from somewhere who have come for a variety of reasons, and perhaps because of that they judge each person individually and accept or reject according to the way you hold up as a human being. I was not prejudged as a member of a race or religion. I was Helen. How I liked that!

Instead of me teaching the "hicks" a thing or two, they helped me to shed some of my own provincialism and prejudices. Once when I stated flatly that I "hated drunks" a student friend from the University of Alaska insisted I attend a meeting of Alcoholics Anonymous. He was right. I came away humbled by the suffering, honesty and courage I had observed, and quite certain I'd never make such a general, unthinking statement again.

Unlike New York, where I had several distinct groups of friends, each suited to a separate part of my personality or interests, my friends in Fairbanks overlapped from one group to another. That may be because of the relatively small population there, or because many of my new friends had similar interests. What makes the people in Fairbanks interesting, I think, is their willingness to compare backgrounds and experiences.

I certainly got to know people with all kinds of backgrounds and experiences—from American farm girls to European war refugees, from boys who ran away from home at the age of sixteen to girls, like me, who had never been away from home before, from artists and intellectuals to technicians and the SAC commanders and GI's, bush pilots and gold prospectors. Perhaps it was because I allowed myself to become involved in the lives of others for the first time that I became both friendly with and close to so many wonderful people. I also received a few shocks, because within my first few months in Fairbanks I observed the trials, tragedies and traumas of illicit love affairs, promiscuity, abortion and (of all things for such a predominantly male country) lesbianism. I became more aware of how naïve I actually was, experiencing things that previously I had only heard and read about in New York. I also learned to stop judging people by preconceived standards of behavior and morals. I found that, while not necessarily approving of or even condoning various actions, I still could be and, indeed, was terribly fond of the people involved.

There was something marvelously liberating about making friends. I felt taken out of myself and my problems—real and imaginary. I think I actually blossomed. And perhaps it was this blossoming that permitted me to fall in love for the first time in my life. When I started for Alaska, I knew I was searching for Experience, but I didn't know what kinds of experiences I was looking for. Perhaps subconsciously I *was* looking for Love, because I did feel I was incapable of loving anyone or being able to make anyone love me, but I know I did not go to Alaska for the specific purpose of falling in love. Yet that is exactly what happened to me in Fairbanks, and it was the most beautiful and important thing that has happened in my life so far—giving love and receiving love in return. I know that the ability to offer myself and the capacity to accept the gift of another —these revelations of love transformed me into a better person, into another person altogether. For the first time, I saw the possibilities of life, the possibilities of my part in life, of marrying and raising a family. For the rest of my life, when I remember Fairbanks, I will remember my first love. What nicer thing could anyone remember or say about any place?

By the middle of January I felt myself getting restless again. Although I still found my job pleasant enough and my new friends both interesting and congenial, I remembered now that I had come to Alaska in the first place because I wanted to travel. I couldn't remain loyal to my job and travel at the same time, and the weather in Alaska was too bad for traveling and would remain so for the next few months. So it seemed time to move on.

I had several alternate plans. A friend of mine had a cabin in the woods about twenty miles outside Fairbanks that he wasn't using and I thought I could live in it. I thought it might be fine to live off by myself in the woods, and accomplish all the things I wanted: painting and writing. I would take an Alaskan Husky puppy along for company, and that way overcome my fear of animals. Then another friend of mine knew some girls in San Francisco who were planning a trip to Mexico, and I thought that sounded like fun. I wanted to go to San Francisco anyway, and I thought that after I came back from Mexico, I might go to Hong Kong, get a job there, then keep on going around the world.

So on January 17 I gave the Bureau of Land Management two weeks' notice and started getting ready to leave Fairbanks on February 1. I decided against the cabin in the woods and for San Francisco. There was a commercial airline flight from Fairbanks to San Francisco that left at 11 A.M. on Friday, February 1, and I thought I'd probably take it.

Sunday I was looking over all the stuff I had accumulated in my five months in Fairbanks, trying to decide what to pack, what to ship, and what to give away, when I heard a commercial announcement on the radio. The pilot of a small plane was flying to San Francisco, and was looking for a passenger to share expenses. I responded just as I had to the two ads in *The New York Times*. This was for me!

I had been in a small plane only once before. A friend of mine, a bush pilot, had given me a ride over

Fairbanks one afternoon. He even let me fly the plane myself a little. It was very exciting, and only a little scary. I thought flying in a little plane to San Francisco would be much more fun than in one of the passenger planes that fly so high you never get to see anything but clouds below. Besides, I thought, this flight would be cheaper than the commercial flight.

When they announced the telephone number, I wrote it down, but lost the slip of paper. Monday there was no announcement, so I assumed he'd found his passenger. Then on Tuesday I heard the ad again, and this time I called. The number was for a Fairbanks rooming-house. The pilot wasn't there, but his landlady was taking calls for her friend, Mr. Flores, and she gave me a lot of information. The plane was a five-seater, and the pilot wanted to leave as soon as possible. He would fly from Fairbanks to the San Carlos airport outside San Francisco via Whitehorse in the Yukon and Fort Nelson in British Columbia. The passenger's share of the expenses was only $70, or about half what the airline ticket would cost.

"When does he want to leave?" I asked.

"Wednesday."

"Oh, I'll never be ready in time," I said. "Besides, I promised to finish out the week on my job."

I thought no more about it until my telephone rang Thursday evening. It was the pilot, Ralph Flores. His voice was soft and he spoke with an accent I assumed was Spanish.

"I've been held up by the weather," he said, "and I

can't get off till tomorrow after all. Are you still interested?"

I said I was.

He said he'd come around to my place that evening and look at my baggage to see what kind of load he'd have.

Ralph arrived a little ahead of time, and seemed very rushed and preoccupied. He told me not to fly with him unless I trusted him, and I—despite the reservations of some of my friends who felt it was a bad time of the year to fly over such rough, desolate country with a pilot I didn't know anything about—said I did trust him. Since I didn't know anything about planes or what kind of equipment they should have, I didn't know what kind of questions to ask him, anyway. But one of my friends, a private pilot, told me that in the same circumstances he'd go himself, if the pilot was a good one.

When I lit a cigarette, Ralph stared at me in an odd way, and said, "Smoke all you want now. You can't smoke on the plane." I didn't realize then that smoking was against his religion.

Then Ralph looked over my luggage and almost flipped. "Does this *all* go?"

"No. Just the four bags."

I had decided to take mostly only those things I would need and use in San Francisco and warmer climates and leave behind all my strictly Alaskan gear: the thermal underwear, my heavy boots, and the sleeping bag that I'd brought along in the car on the trip with

Sue. I have since had plenty of opportunity to regret that I left all those warm things behind.

"It's good I have no other passengers," he said, grabbing my biggest suitcase and taking it out to his car.

Ralph took me to the boardinghouse to meet his landlady, Margot Blevins. She told me what a fine man and good pilot he was. "You're in wonderful hands," she kept saying. Margot told me a little about Ralph. He was Mexican, had just finished more than a year as a mechanic on the DEW line, and was going home to his family in California.

Ralph drove me back to my apartment, and told me he'd pick me up at 8:30 the next morning.

"How about food?" I asked. "Should I bring some sandwiches?"

"If you want, you can bring something. Just in case."

I had fallen back into my old habit of compulsive eating during the last few months in Fairbanks, and I was heavy: 140 pounds. I decided the five-day trip to San Francisco would be a perfect time to start dieting. Instead of making sandwiches, I took what fresh fruit I had in my apartment, a few apples and oranges and Tang.

Ralph arrived the next morning with a Mexican-born woman, a friend of his, who drove us to the airfield. I was dressed in a turtleneck sweater, under an insulated sweatshirt with a hood. On top of that was my parka. I had on wool slacks over red stretch tights, two pairs of wool socks and rainboots. I had two big handbags and my four suitcases: a small red case filled with lingerie; a green soft-sided suitcase packed with nothing but sweaters (I had written home so much about the cold that my mother had kept sending me new sweaters and heavy socks); a dress bag filled with dresses and coats; and the heavy suitcase that Ralph had taken the night before.

What with loading and fueling the plane, we didn't get off till 11:30. The weather was clear and cold—about 30 below zero. In fact, it was one of the clearest days I had seen all winter in Fairbanks. Ralph was working in just a white dress shirt and a leather jacket. He had a big, handsome wolf-and-fox parka, but he wasn't wearing it. He had on rubber boots and wool slacks. He tied down two of my cases in the luggage compartment, then set the other two loose in the back seat.

I asked him how old his plane was.

He smiled, and said, "Your age."

I thought twenty-one seemed pretty old for an airplane—I knew it would be for a car—but my bush-pilot friend had told me that as long as a plane was kept in good condition, it didn't really matter how old it was.

While I was waiting for Ralph to finish fueling, I saw a man I had known in Fairbanks. We chatted awhile, and I told him about the trip.

"Oh," he said, "I see you're going with old Ralph Flores."

He walked away without explaining just what he meant. I wondered if I should have asked more about my pilot, but both Margot at the roominghouse and the

Mexican woman who had driven us out seemed to have a very high regard for him.

There was something curious about Ralph. As I watched him working around the plane, I had a hunch he wasn't really such a quiet man; he just didn't have much he cared to say to most people. It was almost as if he felt a little superior—or removed. He was obviously very independent. When other men went by and tried to give him a hand, he just said "yes" or "no" and walked away. He didn't seem to want to accept anyone's help.

I was almost sorry when Ralph finally called to me that we were ready to take off. It was such an incredibly beautiful day after so many gloomy ones. I hadn't seen all I wanted to of Alaska by any means. It had frustrated me to be weathered and not able to keep moving around and doing things. As I climbed into the plane, I promised myself I'd come back.

Ralph saw I was properly settled into the seat beside him, showed me how to work the seat belt and handed me the maps. Then we took off, rushing into the clear, glittering winter air in a smooth arc. I looked down over Fairbanks with a feeling of nostalgia. So much had happened to me there. I had learned a good deal about other people and myself. I knew it would always be vivid to me.

I poked Ralph, pointed down excitedly. "Look, there's where I lived."

As we left Fairbanks and flew out over open country, Ralph pointed out the lakes and rivers on the map, and told me to watch for them below. At first it was fun, staring down at the terrain spread out beneath us. I had drawn a lot of it on my job. But after a while it was all alike, with no points of interest, and I got sleepy. It was too noisy to try to talk—even if my pilot had been a talkative man.

We arrived at Whitehorse around four that afternoon, just as it was getting dusk. Ralph got the plane berthed for the night and we went into town to the Taku Hotel. We had a snack—soup and a sandwich—in the hotel coffee shop. When the food was placed before us, and I started to pick up my soup spoon, Ralph stopped me.

"Before we eat, let's pray."

It was all right with me. We both bent our heads, and I waited. But his prayer was silent.

After supper we played checkers. I drew a diagram of a checkerboard on a piece of paper, and made makeshift checkers out of coins. During the checker game I tried to find out a little more about this strange man, and he seemed eager to tell me about his life. At one point he mentioned that he was the father of seven children. That puzzled me, for Margot had said he had six.

"I thought you had six," I said.

"The first one was by another marriage," he said. "That child is living in Mexico."

He went on to explain he had been born in a small village near Mexico City and raised a Catholic. He had married a village girl when he was very young. Later, he divorced his wife and came to the United States alone as a migrant fruit picker, working in Washington and California, following the crops. Eventually he trained as a mechanic, remarried—a Mexican woman he met in San Francisco. Four years ago, after his father's death, Ralph had become a convert to the Mormon church, and he and his wife and children were all devout Mormons.

It was an interesting story, but I had difficulty following it because of his accent, and I had to ask him to repeat things. Besides, I was very tired, and Ralph didn't play a good enough game of checkers to keep me awake. After a while, I excused myself and went to sleep.

The next morning Ralph woke me at 6 A.M. We dressed, and then Ralph called the airport and found the weather past Teslin was below the minimum safe flying conditions, although Whitehorse itself was all right.

"We'll have to wait till it clears ahead."

I grumbled to myself, wondering why he hadn't called about the weather *before* we got dressed. We had breakfast in the coffee shop, and then I gave Ralph a tour of the town. After an hour or so of walking around, I realized I'd made a mistake about those boots. My rainboots simply weren't warm enough for subzero weather.

We found two movie theaters in town, and went into one to kill time. It was Walt Disney's *Nanook of the Northwest* and five cartoons. I remembered how I used to love cartoons, and thinking as a child that I'd always stay young and enjoy cartoons. But it wasn't true any more; I thought they were silly. At least my feet were warm.

When we came out of the show, I bought a portable checker set and a copy of the poems and prose of Robert Service. By now, having spent two days with Ralph, I liked him well enough, but I found it almost impossible to discuss anything with him because he seldom understood what I was talking about, and I had a hard time following him. That night we went to the other movie.

Sunday morning was beautiful in Whitehorse, but when Ralph checked on the weather there was still no clearance. He suggested we take a walk out to the airport, which was several miles outside town. I was determined to lose some weight, and Ralph was somewhat overweight himself. On the way out, I realized how strong Ralph was. He kept up a steady pace and never seemed to tire. I fell back a couple of times, completely beat, but he kept right on trudging along. By the time we reached the field my feet were wet right through, and I was so tired we agreed to take a cab back.

While we were out there we poked around the plane and Ralph got out some frozen chicken he had along. We took it back to the hotel, put it on the radiator to thaw, and ate it for supper. I'm not very fond of chicken, so there were a couple of pieces left that we took out to the plane the next day. That night we went to another movie (they changed the bill on Sundays).

The next morning we flew off into the storm. . . .

X

... The more I thought about the Bible and my family during those days I spent alone in the plane while the storm raged outside the more I realized the most important rule to me was not stated directly in the Ten Commandments, but certainly implied. It was the one about hurting someone deliberately. Of all my sins, the one that distressed me the most was my indifference to my little sister Linda. She had always loved me. Yet I had often been mean to her. I'd refused to lend her my clothes. I wouldn't help her with her schoolwork. I wouldn't exchange confidences with her, or help her with things I'd already experienced. And I had fought with her.

The more it preyed upon my mind the more I condemned myself for hurting Linda. She was the one I had sinned most against. Perhaps she, through her forgiveness, was the only one who could save me. So again, as I had done weeks before, I tried to talk to my sister. Only this time I prayed.

"Love me, Linda," I prayed over and over. "Love me."

And Linda heard me. Not consciously, or in a dream. But my prayers somehow shaped Linda's prayers. I found out later that Linda, like my mother, never gave up hope that I was alive. "I love you, Helen," Linda called out to me each night I was missing. "I love you."

The weather at the crash site continued bad, but at least the blizzard had stopped. The three days Ralph had expected to be gone came and passed. And then four . . . and five. I didn't really worry. If Ralph had survived the blizzard—and somehow I felt he had—then he might have found the highway he'd thought he'd seen, and started walking toward civilization. If he was alive, he'd be back for me. If he didn't come back? Well, if it ever got warm again, I thought I'd bundle my feet as best I could, and try to follow his tracks, if the snow hadn't erased them all. It still didn't really occur to me that I might die, that I might freeze, that I might be starving to death.

Once, when the wind came and blew the snow away for a few hours, I ventured outside. I was inching around, looking things over, guiding my steps by holding on to the plane, when my hand hit something on top of the fuselage that made me pause and look. It was a wad of chewing gum. I clawed it off the plane and popped it into my mouth. Our chewing-gum supply had run out long ago. But when I'd finished mine, I'd thrown it away. Frugal Ralph had stored his for the future. It was frozen hard, but after I gnawed at it a few minutes it began to melt. I felt as elated as though I'd just discovered a frozen five course TV dinner. I didn't think Ralph would mind my using his gum.

I was thinking about my mother all the time now, and I found myself talking to her. "Ma!" I'd say. "Listen to me. Ma, I'm alive! I'm alive, Ma!" Thinking about my mother made me think about her wishes for me to get married and have a family of my own. So I started concentrating on a possible husband, and how I should go about trapping him. For some reason (maybe because I was always looking for job ads in *The New York Times*) I saw myself back in New York again, looking in the Help Wanted section of the *Times*, and there was an ad for someone to fill a diversified job—no skills required. I would be one out of a whole lot of applicants, and that was how I would meet this fellow. He would be sharp and rugged like the men I had met in Fairbanks. In comparison, the men in New York seem less masculine but perhaps more intelligent—more articulate, anyway. But this fellow would be both—sharp and rugged. Big wedding, champagne, tears. And then, just as my mother wanted, I would have a baby.

As the days faded into each other, I was increasingly convinced God was keeping me there for a purpose. I hadn't realized what my sins were until I was alone. But now I couldn't understand why God was making my mother suffer. I knew she could never have done anything so terrible, and I knew how upset she must be. I didn't feel God was punishing me, but I kept wondering if I was doing what He wanted. So I promised myself and God that if I got out alive, I would become a more directed, more purposeful person. After several days of thought, I also decided to promise myself and God to eat less. But somehow that didn't seem enough.

In one of our discussions, Ralph had quoted from the Bible something that had puzzled me at the time: "Faith without works is dead." Perhaps I should be doing something specific, but I still wasn't sure what it was.

I did feel reading the Bible was part of what God wanted me to do, because my compulsion was so strong to finish it. Just as I'd had a powerful compulsion to leave home and then later to leave Fairbanks. I'd listened those times and followed what I felt was my direction.

If God did decide to let me live, what would I do? It was one thing to promise Him things in these drastic circumstances, but I wondered if when I got back home and my life filled up with normal, everyday activities I would forget Him. More than ever I wanted to grasp firmly and keep holding on to my feeling of blessedness. Perhaps that was why I was here. I didn't really know.

When I did pray, I felt I was answered; not with a vision but with a sense of comfort. I felt very safe and curiously tranquil. Ralph had been gone a week now, but I still did not feel overly concerned for him or even for myself. I felt a deepening patience and faith within me. I felt I was experiencing God.

I had never read the New Testament before. There were several things new to me that I liked and borrowed. One was the Holy Ghost. From Judaism I remembered the Holy Spirit that I suppose is different from the Christian Holy Ghost, but I leave that to the theologians to argue. I just *liked* the Holy Ghost. I liked the idea of asking to be filled with the spirit of the Holy Ghost, which was to me the spirit of God within you, the spirit of Love. I prayed God would fill me with the Holy Ghost, that He would show Himself to me in some way, and bless me, even as He had Abraham, Jacob and Isaac.

As I had told Ralph, I did not pray in the conventional sense of saying a prayer, but just talked to my friend God. Now I felt it would be consoling to have a special prayer to say as my own. I looked through the Bible to find a prescribed prayer I liked, and I came to the part where Jesus was telling people how to pray. I read the prayer he taught them: "Our Father, who art in Heaven . . ."

I liked the sound of that, and there was nothing in

it to conflict with anything I believed. "Hallowed be Thy Name . . ." Then I got to "Thy Kingdom come," and, after puzzling over the phrase for some time, I decided I wasn't at all sure what it meant. So since I didn't want to pray just words, I cut that line out. "Thy Will be done." I felt very strongly I was placed where I was at God's will. And it would only be by His will that I would be released. "On earth as it is in Heaven." I certainly felt that, for my God is everywhere.

When I came to "Give us this day our daily bread" I confess it made me laugh. It seemed so ridiculous to ask for bread when I hadn't eaten for weeks, and at that moment was savoring an ancient, frozen piece of chewing gum. Besides, I'd never liked asking God for personal favors. Rather I would say to Him, "I want to go home, *if* it is Your will." I always thought it was presumptuous of anyone to ask God to give him something special for himself. Once when I said that to Ralph, he replied, "Ask and ye shall receive, seek and ye shall find." But I still believed God would nourish me as He saw fit. For "daily bread" I substituted the words: "Give us strength."

"And forgive us our trespasses as we forgive those who trespass against us." Yes. If I truly tried to be compassionate toward people and understand their treatment of me, surely I could ask God to understand me, too. Now I also remember a passage I had come upon in Matthew. "Judge not, that ye be not judged." How directly those words seemed to apply to me! I wished I might have come upon those words years before.

"And lead us not into temptation..." No, I could not accept that, because I did not truly believe it. I had never wished to be shielded from life or troubles or my own weaknesses. I felt God could lead me into all the temptation He wanted, and then test my will not to transgress. For me life is and must be experience. How do you grow unless you see things, taste things and learn, perhaps painfully, what is bad for you? I could not pray to be protected from life, particularly in my present position.

"Give me a chance to repent," I asked. "Give me a chance at life again; a chance to accomplish something, to produce something. Let me go home. *Let me live!*"

XI

It was about 3 P.M. of the eighth day I had been alone. Another gray, depressing day in which I'd stayed wrapped in my blanket inside the plane. I had not even bothered to try and melt some water for the last two days. When I had prayed that morning, I had asked God for "just a little miracle. Not a big one, Lord. Just a little one"; that He be with Ralph and protect him. Not for me, but for our families.

Now I was reading one of the Psalms of David:

How long, O Jehovah, wilt Thou forget me for ever? How long wilt Thou hide thy face from me?

I sat up, thinking I had heard an odd sound, like a call. I listened, then went back to the Bible. My ears were so bad now that I could hear little. Then I stopped reading again; I *had* heard something. I threw back the tarpaulin that covered the door, and listened, my head outside the plane.

It was a cry. "Helen!" Ralph's voice. Far off in the woods.

I started to jump out of the plane and go to him. Then I stopped, remembering how he'd fuss at me for getting my sore feet filled with snow. I made myself sit back and wait, crying with relief. It was nearly a half hour later when Ralph trudged into the clearing.

I was so happy I jumped out of the plane and hugged and kissed him, laughing and crying all at the same time. My "little miracle" had been answered.

Ralph made a fire, started boiling up some water and even sang a few songs in Spanish to me. He seemed smaller than when he had left; shrunken, gnomelike. I realized what the trip had cost him. But Ralph was fired with plans. He hadn't reached the sound, but he had found a place to which he felt we should move. "You'll love it, Helen," he kept saying, his voice alive with excitement. "It's in a clearing where you can see the whole sky. Not far from the lake. You'll love it, Helen. You really will." He sounded like a loving father describing a vacation resort to his daughter.

Ralph had worked his way downhill from our mountainside and found a clearing he felt would make a good campsite. He had made a shelter for us there, and then waited, hoping a plane would sight him. But no plane ever appeared, so he decided to come back for me, after first exploring the lake. Ralph wanted us to move down to the clearing, where our camp would be more visible from the air, before he tried to go on farther and follow the sound.

The site was, he thought, "about two miles" downhill from where we were. Ralph was anxious to move immediately, but the weather was forbidding. Besides, we had to decide what we would take with us and how we would carry it. And how I would move. Ralph thought he could make a toboggan and load our belongings on it. I could sit on it, and he would pull or push the whole thing.

The next day we made our preparations to move. We also lined the floor and the sides of the plane cabin with spruce boughs, which made our little haven more comfortable and warmer than it had ever been. It was so wonderful to have Ralph back, yet I was shocked at myself to realize I was less at ease now than when I had been alone. Then the plane had been like a snug, private cabin where I could lie in my cocoon and think and do as I pleased. Now I was the housewife again who had to share the blanket, keep up the interior—and go outside to the bathroom again.

It snowed all day on March 16, the day after Ralph returned, but we kept busy, preparing for our trip, anyway. When I showed Ralph the little clock that had let me down, he fixed it within a few minutes. He made a toboggan out of part of the fuselage and a piece of spruce. We decided to take the cushions from the plane, the sleeping bag I'd made, a strip of fabric with the plane's identification number, engine cover, coats, cans, clothes. Ralph had two metal suitcases but decided they were too heavy. Instead, we filled my fabric dress bag with sweaters and coats. As I had lost weight, and my clothes fell more slackly on my body, letting in air drafts, I had added more clothes to keep warm. By now I was wearing four pairs of pants—two of my own and two I had wheedled out of Ralph—and four sweaters. Ralph thought my camera was too heavy to bother with, but I took it anyway, since it belonged to my sister. I took my make-up case and Ralph his shaving kit, since we both wanted to look our best when we got home.

I was supposed to sit on the back of the loaded toboggan, since I had no snowshoes, but when we had it piled high and I sat on it, it was far too heavy either to pull or push. I got off, and it was still immovable. Ralph cut the toboggan in half, and we reloaded, leaving much of our original load behind.

We were finally ready to leave around 3 P.M. on what I thought was March 17, but I have since reconstructed my chronology and learned that often I was one or two days off. Anyway, it had stopped snowing, though the skies had not cleared and it was bitterly cold. The last thing I did before leaving the site was paint a directional sign on the plane. The sign, painted with my red oil paints, was to direct anyone who might find the plane before they found us.

WENT

⟶

2 MI.

DOWN HILL

3/16/63

Since Ralph could not pull me on the sled, he fixed my feet for walking by wrapping them with extra canvas, which he roped to my legs. He put me in front, with a rope over my good shoulder, to steer the sled. Ralph pushed from behind.

He told me to walk in his old tracks that he had made coming back to the plane. I tried, but it had snowed since then and half the time I fell through. Once I got started I could keep my feet moving, but if anything stopped me I found I could not pick up my right foot. Ralph had to come around to the front and lift it for me. Then I could move forward again till I went through the snow or stumbled. Each time my foot went down in the deep snow the ropes that held the canvas came undone. With only one functioning arm, it was impossible for me to retie them. Ralph had to come and tie them for me, then get me started again.

He wasn't in much better shape than I was. Our load was simply too heavy to pull wearing snowshoes, so Ralph took them off, piled them on top of the sled, and floundered in and out of drifts as I was doing, falling almost as often.

We couldn't synchronize our movements. When Ralph gave a push from the back, the momentum caused me to fall forward, sometimes to my knees. Our trail led us through deep snow, in and out of steep gullies full of brush, trees, windfall logs. Even with good feet to walk on, it would have been murderous.

I tasted bile in my mouth and felt as though I might vomit. I wanted to sink down in the snow and just rest and get my breath back, but I couldn't keep Ralph waiting. Finally we came to a dead stop midway up a small, steep hill when I fell down and the toboggan went over with me. Ralph—ever patient, determined, steady— decided it was not balanced properly, so he took everything off, got it reloaded, then reroped it, while I sat in the snow gasping.

We hit another hill so steep I would not have tried to ski down it. I couldn't help Ralph with the weight; the most I could do was steer a little with the lead rope over my good shoulder. We got up somehow but, going downhill, Ralph expected me to go ahead and guide the sled. I couldn't. I didn't have enough balance to hold myself, let alone the sled. I tried to walk down—and fell end over end, rolling the length of the hill. If I were in New York in Central Park, I thought, I'd call this fun.

When my body stopped turning, I looked back and saw Ralph coming down fast, around bushes and trees, trying to brake the toboggan from behind so it wouldn't run away from him. I hated myself for not being able to help him, but I could hardly help myself. I couldn't recall ever experiencing such agonizing exhaustion.

It took us five hours to make the run of "about two miles" that was actually, I later learned, less than three-quarters of one mile. The last fifty yards in failing light —uphill to a knoll—were the worst. Now Ralph was pulling the sled and I was trying to push, but I had no leverage in the deep snow. The only thing I could push with was my belly. I thrust it against the sled and pushed with all the strength I could summon. The sled went a little way, then stopped. We couldn't get it moving again.

Ralph decided to take some of our things off the toboggan and carry them up the hill to the campsite in the clearing. It was dark now, and he was soon out of sight. I just sank down in the snow, waiting for him to come back. The canvases had slipped off my feet and I couldn't retie them. I couldn't go on. I knew if Ralph didn't come back for me, I would never get up again.

Ralph did come back, and told me to follow right behind him. We both carried some more stuff from the toboggan. When we finally got to the top of the knoll, I slipped down to the ground and just lay there. I couldn't move; I couldn't breathe. My mind was still clear but my body was gone. I watched Ralph push away the snow from the lean-to he'd built before when he was living in the clearing, feeling guilty that I was just lying there when there was so much work to do. I wanted water in the most terrible way, yet I didn't want to ask him to stop and fix it.

Then I began to throw up. There was nothing in my stomach—except its own secretions. There was bile, a terrible, thick, green, vile-tasting fluid that ran from the corners of my mouth. When he heard me retching, Ralph stopped his work and came over to me and held my head.

He had not wanted to build a fire because the fire-light would blot out our faint trail marks in the dark, and he had to make other trips back to the toboggan. Now he made one quick trip back, then got a fire going, boiled water and brought me some. Nothing in my life ever tasted so good. The next thing Ralph did was to take the soaked sweaters off my feet and dry them over the fire. He bound my feet with rags torn out of one of my cotton nightgowns we'd taken along on the toboggan for just that purpose.

All this revived me somewhat; enough, anyway, to enable me to help him fix up our shelter for the night. Moving very slowly, we stretched a tarpaulin on the ground, placed the cushions and blanket on top of that, and settled in. It was about 11:30 P.M.

The next morning it was cloudy but not snowing. I looked around at my new home with something less than elation. When Ralph had kept saying "you'll love it," I had envisioned a pretty, open site framed with tall pines and spruce. This *was* an open knoll, looking out over a valley that we later learned was part of the Rocky Mountain Trench, but there had been a forest fire. The trees were all black and scorched limbs stretched to the gray sky. It reminded me of one of those Smokey the Bear ads that warn against starting forest fires.

I looked around, shuddered, and said to Ralph, "It looks like death."

"You can see the sky," he said.

It was true. I glanced up and found the whole horizon awaiting me. If a plane came over this spot, you certainly could see it. Also, here, with no danger of gasoline explosion, we could have our fire right in front of our tent where we could use it for warmth as well as a signal twenty-four hours a day.

Ralph staggered off down the slope and hauled the toboggan back up to our clearing. Then he got his hammer and chisel out of his toolbox and started hacking away at the trees again. For two days Ralph worked, cutting up a wood supply for the fire and improving our shelter. He used the toboggan standing on its end as one wall and wired it together with poles and limbs. Over the top and along the sides Ralph hung pieces of canvas and wired and roped these to a crossbar and to the poles. We made a crude sort of floor out of some more limbs and on top of these we placed a lot of spruce boughs. As I watched Ralph labor away, it suddenly occurred to me that he'd had nothing to eat for—I counted up—over thirty days. Even then, his strength and endurance seemed unbelievable.

While we worked Ralph told me that, as soon as he was rested from our trek, he was going on down to the beaver lake he had found, and make an S.O.S. in the snow in the meadow beside it, since bush pilots always look at the water markers along their routes. Then, he said, he would go on toward the sound we'd been hearing.

I seemed to have left my feeling of safety and comfort at the wrecked plane. There was something eerie about this place that made me uneasy. I looked around at the charred black fingers of the trees and the bleak white snow. There was nothing alive.

"I saw tracks of large animals on the way here," I told Ralph.

"Probably just a bunch of rabbits."

"No, they were big paw marks. Much bigger than a rabbit's." I looked at him, not wanting to plead, but I was afraid. "I don't want to be alone here."

"It won't be for long," he said. "You'll be safe with a big fire going. Even if there are large animals, they won't come up to the fire. I've got to get on down there and make that signal where it's sure to be seen."

Ralph looked off toward the lake, his eyes fixed in their private plan. I realized it was for the best. Then he started telling me again I'd be rescued when I accepted the divinity of Christ. I just listened. Ralph said he was now more certain than ever that it was his mission to convert me to Christianity, so that I would be an example to the Jewish people.

I said nothing. I wondered if he was really strong enough to go on. He had visibly wasted since he first left me. His once-stocky body was now a skinny frame on which the conglomeration of sweaters and jackets hung loosely. His face was thin and sunken; the eye above the injured cheekbone had a wild look.

"Yes, but first you must rest," I said finally.

"I'll rest today," he said. "It's too cloudy to go on. But if the weather is all right tomorrow, I'll leave."

The rest of that day Ralph spent gathering enough wood to last me for two days. But for hours, on and off, he was seized by violent attacks of abdominal cramps that left him doubled up in the snow. I had never seen Ralph cry before, but now I watched him stop chiseling wood when the spasms attacked him, and stand there, his arms around his belly, tears streaking down through the dirt and stubble of his face. He had held me when I vomited. I tried to think of something I could do for him. In the end, I started reading the Bible aloud to him while he clutched himself.

That afternoon I sat by the fire and unbandaged my feet. I knew the trip had aggravated them, possibly stirred up a new infection. I found both feet were running a mucuslike fluid and they had that terrible smell now. I could see clearly the ends of bone protruding through the black crust of the right foot. I held it up and showed it to Ralph. "Do you think I'll lose my toes?" I asked him. "Do you think my toes will fall off?" I wasn't thinking of possible surgical amputation. I just thought if they really died completely, they'd drop off my foot, like overripe fruit.

"No," Ralph said. "They'll be all right, daughter. They won't fall off."

"Okay, Daddy-O, if you say so."

I tore up fresh bandages and tied up my feet, so we could both forget about them.

When the next day dawned clear, I knew Ralph would leave, regardless of anything I might say. He had the look in his eye of a man absolutely possessed. It was as if he were deliberately spending his last measure of strength—or perhaps summoning a strength he didn't have himself but that was inspired.

I didn't say any more about not wanting to be left alone. I'd got along before. I would have to make my own peace again.

Then we heard the noise around noon. It sounded closer from here. To Ralph it was a good omen. He strapped on his snowshoes, tied his pack on his back, put the binoculars around his neck, and took the compass and his spear in his hands. Then, with my silly hat still on his head, he started out once more.

Again I sat by the fire, watching and calling after him, my eyes misted with tears. He was so weak now.

It was, I thought, March 20. I wrote in my notebook. "Ralph left . . . please, God, be with him."

XII

This time the little plane clock kept running, and the weather remained fair. In fact, my apprehensions about this eerie new camp proved groundless. It was more comfortable in the canvas tent, with the fire right in front of the opening, than it had been inside the plane. And I didn't really have to worry about wood, for in addition to what Ralph left me, there were plenty of fallen trees and branches lying around the edge of the clearing that I could drag to the fire when I needed it.

I neither saw nor heard any of the large animals I feared so. Occasionally a bird would sing in the trees, and whenever I heard one I had a feeling of complete gratitude—toward the bird, and God too. I lay in the sun with my blanket around me, close enough to the fire to be warm, a can of water close by, and the sun and blue sky overhead. I couldn't ask for anything more except my family.

Most of my daylight hours were spent reading and thinking. In fact, the sun was so bright I got out my pair of prescription sun glasses. My ordinary reading glasses had been broken in the crash, but I had gotten along perfectly well without them—with no headaches at all. I was nearly finished with the Bible, and putting it down, I thought again of Tolstoy's "The Death of Ivan Ilych."

The thing that struck me the most forcibly as I recalled the story was the fact that Ivan was the only one who actually knew he was dying. He could not communicate with those standing around him—his wife, his friend, even his doctor. He alone knew of his imminent death, just as he alone recognized the emptiness of the life he had lived. It occurred to me that, limited as my life was, it had not been that empty. I had been able to enjoy and appreciate many things. In contrast to Ivan, I had at least tried to experience Life. What I wanted most now was a chance to do something with what I had experienced. I compared my present lot to Ivan's. He was bedridden for three weeks; I was almost bedridden. He was wracked with constant pain; I only hurt in spasms and when I tried to stand, or when my feet got terribly cold. On the other hand, Ivan was not slowly starving to death; yet I wasn't even terribly hungry these days. It seemed to me that I was much better off than poor Ivan.

Although I had little idea of when Ralph would return, I was not particularly disturbed. I had wood and water, and I was more comfortable than I had been since we crashed. It was odd how each new thing we learned brought us additional comfort: the boiling of the water, the making of the insulated blanket, and now this tent. I didn't know how long I could last, but I didn't feel I was dying. Except for my feet, Ralph was now in worse shape than I was, and he certainly wasn't giving up.

Ralph's plan was to go down to the lake, which he had estimated was no more than three miles from the camp (it turned out to be four miles), tramp an S.O.S. in the snow on the level land nearby, then proceed in the direction of our noise, and try to locate either its source or a highway. Ralph had concluded the noise must come from a lumber or mining camp, and since such remote camps often have only once- or twice-a-week contact with the outside world, we had estimated that even after he got there, it might be another week or more before help could be sent back to me.

I was sorry I could not see the lake from where I was. Ralph seemed so certain someone was bound to spot the S.O.S. he was going to make. The very last thing he said to me before he left was, "When they come for you,

Helen, don't let them give up the search until they have found me too." It was what he had said when he left me the first time. Ralph had saved my life a dozen times in the weeks gone by. I was not about to leave him out there to die.

Ralph left on Thursday. I later learned it took him about six hours to get down to the meadow, which turned out to be a frozen swamp. Wearing his snowshoes, he stamped an enormous S.O.S.—each letter about seventy-five feet long. Then he stamped out a long arrow pointing back in direction of where I was. That night he made a fire, boiled some water, and went to sleep in my coat on top of a bed of spruce boughs he had cut and chiseled down.

The next day, Friday, Ralph started walking in the direction of the noise and where he thought the highway might be. He walked all day and slept that night in the hollow of a tree. Saturday he climbed up to the top of a seventy-foot tree hoping to find some landmarks. But he didn't see anything recognizable. The climb and the previous day's walking had so exhausted him that he slept in the tree hollow the rest of the day and all through the night. On Sunday he started walking again. That afternoon, as he was crossing a frozen creek, he saw and heard an airplane. Ralph had one of our mirrors with him, and he started signaling with it. The plane circled low around him and then flew away, but Ralph knew he had been sighted.

I read the Bible all day Thursday and finished it on

Friday. Saturday was a beautiful day, and in the morning I heard a plane flying nearby. I stumbled out of the tent and stood in the clearing, scanning the sky, but the plane was evidently on the other side of the mountain, for I couldn't see it. And then it was gone. I crawled back into my warm burrow, and wrote in my diary, "Heard a plane today. God be with us."

Sunday the weather was still fair. I was sitting on a cushion, tending the fire and reading around one o'clock in the afternoon, when I heard another plane. This one sounded closer. I scrambled out of the tent and pulled an armload of pine into the fire to raise smoke. By now the plane was in sight directly overhead. I grabbed the piece of canvas with the identification numbers of the plane on it—N5886—and pulled it away from the fire into the center of the clearing where I hoped it could be seen from the sky. Then I got my mirror and began signaling with it.

The plane circled overhead. The smoke from the green pine was billowing up through the air in thick puffs. I stood up, waving my arms and flashing my mirror. Then, when I couldn't bear to stand another second, I sank down while the plane banked. When it circled overhead, I jumped up again. By now I was crying— from pain and joy. I was sure I had been seen, but it hurt so to stay on my feet.

"So rescue me already," I shouted at the plane. "I can't stand."

The plane flew on. I collapsed on the ground. I had

not seen any signal indicating the pilot had actually spotted me. The plane had simply disappeared—like all the others. Yet I was certain he must have seen me, for why else would he have come back that second time? When he flew away, I told myself he probably couldn't find any place to land and was going back for a helicopter that could come down in the clearing—as I had always dreamed would happen. I told myself it would probably take another hour or more to fly to wherever his home base was, get a helicopter and fly back to me. I forced myself to lie back down in my blanket and wait. Since I had finished reading the New Testament, I went back to the Old, to Isaiah, telling myself I had to read through the whole chapter and finish it.

And many people shall go and say, Come ye, and let us go up to the mountain of the Lord, to the house of the God of Jacob; and he will teach us of his ways, and we will walk in his paths: for out of Zion shall go forth the law, and the word of the Lord from Jerusalem.

And he shall judge among the nations, and shall rebuke many people: and they shall beat their swords into plowshares, and their spears into pruning hooks: nation shall not lift up sword against nation, neither shall they learn war any more.

The pilot of that plane, I later learned from him, was Chuck Hamilton, and he *had* seen me. Or rather, as he told me later, he had seen "something" down there underneath all that billowing smoke—"probably an Indian squaw." The exposed skin of my face and hands was by this time so blackened with grime and wood smoke that I was, apparently, not recognizable as a white woman from the air.

Chuck, with his partner Hal Komish, operates the B.C.–Yukon Charter Flying Service at Watson Lake, Canada, about halfway between Whitehorse and Fort Nelson. That Sunday, March 24, he was flying a passenger, an Indian hunting guide named Jack George, and a load of mail and supplies out to Skook Davidson's Diamond J Ranch at Terminus Mountain, the last of the Rocky Mountain range, which lies in the Rocky Mountain Trench, the great valley that extends from the northern part of the United States into Canada. We had crashed on the last mountain rising out of the valley floor. With a glide of twenty miles in any direction, we would have come out onto open meadow.

As usual, Chuck was watching for landmarks along the route, when he spotted something in a small clearing below. He asked Jack George to confirm what he thought looked like an S.O.S., for it seemed very small from the plane. George agreed, and also noted, as had Chuck, Ralph's arrow. The two men studied the sign, concluding it had probably been put there by Indian trappers. The Indians in these remote mountain areas always put out a signal for the bush pilots when they needed something. Only several weeks before, Chuck had made an unscheduled landing by an Indian trapper's cabin in

answer to a HELP written in the snow. It was a young
mother who wanted fresh milk brought in for her baby.
Usually the signals did not indicate emergencies, but
simply a shortage of supplies.

Chuck circled over the S.O.S. several times, then
picked up the trail of Ralph's snowshoes leading away
from the sign. There was something curious about that
trail, Chuck noticed. They weren't the tracks of regular
snowshoes. Instead, they made an odd horseshoe pattern,
obviously home-made, which meant they belonged to
someone not properly equipped—certainly the under-
statement of the year. Anyway, Chuck followed the
snowshoe trail until he finally spied Ralph, who had
mushed along according to his plan, but had just suffered another abdominal spasm. It had left him so weak
that momentarily he could go no farther. He was just
standing in the snow, leaning on his spear, using all his
strength to remain upright. When Ralph heard the
plane engine overhead, he started signaling frantically
with his mirror. And that was how Chuck, circling lower
and lower, spotted him—first the flashing mirror and
then the figure with a pole. Hamilton and George
thought Ralph was an Indian out trapping or fishing.
They also thought he looked to be in trouble.

Chuck was too heavily loaded to land, but it had
occurred to him that the "Indian fisherman" might have
a companion in the area, so he returned to the S.O.S. and
started following the arrow. It was then that I had heard
the plane engine overhead. But I threw so much pine on

the fire they were unable to see much of anything from the air except smoke. After circling a couple of times, they saw the tent and, finally, me—just a dark figure wreathed in wood smoke. They didn't even see my mirror signals, and concluded it was an Indian camp and I was a squaw, standing by the fire, who probably needed some supplies.

Chuck decided he would come back and try to land nearby after he had unloaded, if it wasn't too dark by then. He flew on, dropped George and his supplies at the Davidson Ranch, then flew back, looking for me.

When I heard the plane engine again, I rushed out into the clearing. Fortunately, this time I had let the fire die down and I didn't have so much smoke that it obliterated everything, as it had done before. As Chuck circled down over the campsite, he now made out the identification numbers from the plane that I had spread out in the middle of the clearing. He read them with a growing sense of shock, recognizing N5886 as the numbers of the long-lost Howard that had disappeared with pilot Flores and passenger Klaben seven weeks before.

Chuck wigwagged his plane's wings at me. When he was certain by my answering wave that I had seen his signal, he flew on toward Airplane Lake. He tried to make radio contact with the airport at Watson Lake to report his extraordinary discovery, but was unable to get through, so he located Ralph along the creek trail and then landed on Airplane Lake near an Indian trappers' cabin that had been occupied all the time. The cabin was only twelve miles from our wrecked plane. It was the trappers' chain saw we'd been hearing so tantalizingly all the while.

Chuck told the two Indian trappers, Charlie Porter and Louis Boya, about Ralph, and asked them to go out and try to find him and bring him in. They set out immediately by dogsled. Since Chuck was not equipped for night flying, he set out immediately for Watson Lake and, upon arrival, notified the Royal Canadian Mounted Police of what he had seen and done.

It was almost five o'clock when the plane left me for the second time. I had been waiting since one, and had very nearly given up hope of his return. But when I saw him waggle his wings at me I realized I had been spotted after all. I was so excited I just fell down and cried. This time I was crying from sheer relief and happiness and thankfulness.

When the plane flew on once again I wondered what was going on. As darkness closed in, I didn't know what to do. Should I stay up and wait for him to come back? Or should I try to get some rest? By eight o'clock it was pitch dark and the plane had still not come back. I sat there, huddled in my blanket, wondering what I would and wouldn't take with me. Not the plane cushions this time, I decided, but I would try to take all the clothes we had brought down to the camp.

I waited another half hour before I went about my nightly routine for what I hoped was the last time: fixing the sweaters and blanket into a bed, unwrapping and drying my feet by the fire, putting on my parka, going to the bathroom. By now I realized it was too dark for a plane to come back. Maybe tomorrow . . .

I lay there and prayed. Then, for the first time, I looked up into the night sky. Always before at night I had covered my face with my sweatshirt because it was so cold. Even my eyes would get cold. Anyway, at the other camp we couldn't see the sky, and if there were any animals roaming about I didn't want to see them. But that night my sweatshirt must have slipped part way off, for I looked up and saw stars.

I never saw so many stars in my life. It was like, I remembered, the Planetarium in New York—a tremendous dark dome of sky with millions of beautiful stars. The stars didn't twinkle. They were fixed points of light that seemed millions and millions of miles away. The sky may have been as beautiful on other clear nights, I realized, but I had never seen it before. I decided to watch until I saw a falling star. Finally I saw one, and I made a wish.

I didn't let myself get too excited. The plane had wigwagged that it saw me, but had not come back. Perhaps it never would. Instead of dreaming of leaving and dredging up pictures of home, I just prayed. Again I promised myself and God that if I were rescued I would be good to my mother and more loving to Linda. I lay there, resting, thoughtful, but not asleep. Finally, toward morning, I dozed.

XIII

At 3 A.M. in Brooklyn, as I lay dozing under the Yukon stars, a neighbor of ours named Joanne Russo was watching a late, late TV movie when it was interrupted for a special news bulletin, announcing the survivors of the lost plane had been sighted. "A Canadian bush pilot has spotted a piece of fuselage with the identification of the long-lost plane. There seemed to be a live person..." Joanne waited for a second newscast to make sure the "live person" was thought to be me. Then she ran next door to the Klaben house to see if anyone was awake. The house was dark, so Joanne went back inside, and called on the telephone to tell my family the news. My family knew I was to be rescued before I was sure of it myself. My mother felt that her faith and confidence had been vindicated. She cried with relief and gratitude.

I awoke to the sound of an airplane engine. It was about 6:30 A.M., barely daylight. I decided the plane couldn't be coming for me, because the search planes we had heard never appeared before eleven o'clock. Nevertheless, as the noise grew louder, I crawled out of my blankets to investigate. My fire had gone out during the night, and I did not bother to build it up now. I hobbled out into the clearing and stared up into the pale early-morning sky.

A small plane came into sight; not the same one as I'd seen yesterday. It headed for my clearing, then circled directly over me. I waved. The pilot reached out of his window and dropped something. As it floated toward the ground, I saw it was a red balloon with a little package at the end of a string. The pilot waved at me, and flew on.

The balloon drifted down and landed in a deep snowdrift at one side of the clearing. I had not yet put my canvases on my feet, and I had only the sweaters wrapped around them, but I couldn't wait till I was properly protected to go to that balloon. I had to touch the proof that someone actually knew I was there. Grabbing up a piece of wood for ballast, I inched my way along a fallen log into the snowdrift. As I reached for the balloon I fell into the deep snow, but I scrambled up quickly, retrieved the balloon, then dragged myself, panting, wet and exhausted, back to the tent.

There was a note wrapped around the package. I tore it open. "Good morning." It was the most charming greeting in the world. "There are two other planes on the way." The package contained a couple of chocolate candy bars, a package of chewing gum and one of cigarettes.

I had thought many times about what I would like to eat first after the long fast, and chocolate candy was not high on my list. Mostly I had thought of something bland, warming, easy to digest—like oatmeal and milk and honey. I wasn't even hungry. I sniffed at the chocolate, and it smelled stale, but I decided I should eat it for energy. It tasted awful and made me thirsty; it was full of marshmallows and peanuts and other stuff. My water had frozen overnight, but there didn't seem any point in making a fire now. As soon as I felt strong enough I began putting things in order, getting my bag and small make-up kit packed. I took off my hand-socks and cleaned my nails. Then I brushed my hair.

About an hour later, a man on snowshoes came walking out of the woods into the clearing. He was a small, pixie-faced man with pointed ears. I didn't know who he was, but it didn't matter. I was too exhausted to walk, but when he came over to where I was sitting, I grabbed him around the neck and hugged and kissed him. I was crying, too, and I kept saying over and over again, "Thank God, thank God, thank God." After forty-nine days, I just sort of let go.

He seemed a little embarrassed and shy. I guess he had not been prepared for my emotional reaction to the mere sight of him. When I stopped crying I told him how much I wanted water. The candy had made my mouth so dry. The wood was ready for the morning fire, so he got it started for me, and thawed my water. He told me rescuers were on the way, and that someone would probably come in by dogsled. That excited me. I had always wanted to go dogsledding when I was in Fairbanks.

He had a camera with him and he asked me if I'd stand near the tent so he could take my picture. (It was the one that later appeared on the cover of *Life* magazine.) I thought I should have a picture of my own. I wasn't likely to have a more memorable moment in my life. I got my camera—the Petroflex 5 I had had in Fairbanks—and asked him to take a picture for me, which he did. From then on, it seemed everyone I met pointed a camera at me and clicked before even saying hello, and I began to realize what a news story the rescue really was.

This first rescuer of mine, I learned later, was not the pilot who had spotted me the day before, but a transport employe from Watson Lake named Jack Mc-Callum. When Chuck Hamilton reported he had sighted our camp, and organized a rescue party to come out in the morning, McCallum decided to jump the gun. He had risen early and taken off ahead and alone in his own private plane. McCallum, an old-hand bush pilot, located the camp without trouble, then landed his plane on a little slough about three miles away and mushed in after me. I asked him if Ralph had been found, but he didn't know.

In about an hour the others appeared—Chuck Hamilton and a man they called Al. When McCallum pointed out which man was Hamilton, I called to Chuck, "I can't get up. Please come sit by me."

He walked over and sat beside me, and I kissed him.

Chuck is a big, fair-haired, quiet-spoken man of about thirty-two, with a nice, easy way about him. He had only had his pilot's license one year and his contract license one month. Chuck had been out of town when Ralph and I crashed, so he had not been in on the early rescue attempts. But since his return, he told me, he had kept his eyes open for any sign of a crash, as had all the pilots flying in the area. When Chuck finally discovered us, he realized he had flown over us at least three or four times—without ever spotting the wrecked plane. If Ralph had not decided to move down to the clearing, and then make the S.O.S. out in the open, we and the wrecked plane would not have been seen until spring when the snows melted. I still think we both would have been alive by spring, but I'm certainly glad I didn't have the chance to wait and find out.

I asked Chuck about Ralph. He told me about sending the Indians for him the previous day. Chuck was sure Ralph was all right. I thanked God—silently now.

The three men were discussing how to get me out the three miles to the planes. Hamilton, since he was the biggest, decided he'd carry me piggyback.

I was horrified. How could he carry me? I thought I still weighed 140 pounds. "I'll walk," I said. "I can't stand on my foot, but once I'm moving forward I can walk."

Hamilton shook his head. "No. If I can carry a moose out of the woods, I can certainly carry you." He put on his snowshoes, and knelt down beside me.

It was a beautiful warm day with a bright sun and blue sky. I took off my big parka and Ralph's red woolen shirt, took off my sweatshirt hood and combed my hair, then climbed on Hamilton's back, feeling silly. I hadn't been piggybacked since I was five years old and my brothers carried me around. I felt big and cumbersome and awkward, but, though I didn't yet know it, I weighed a little less than a hundred pounds. McCallum took my suitcase and briefcase with the camera in it; Al carried my black leather sling pocketbook and make-up kit.

Hamilton got me balanced across his broad back, then started out. "You okay?" he asked.

"Sure," I said.

"You better be. They've spent over a million and a half dollars looking for you."

It was a painful trip back to the plane for both of

us, but more for Chuck, I think, than for me. Since my thighs were pinioned under his arms, my legs kept falling asleep. I'd stand it as long as I could, then we'd have to stop and rest awhile. It was a rough trail, crisscrossed with windfall logs. Hamilton's snowshoes would drag and snag on the fallen branches, and he went down several times. But he never hurt me, for when he felt himself going he sank straight down on his knees, so I remained anchored on his back and never fell forward. He told me each time he fell he heard a "little gasp," and was surprised I didn't cry out in pain. The trip took us three hours. I think I remember crying a little—from relief and exhaustion and happiness—and I also talked to Chuck about my mother. I know I was thinking about her.

When we reached the slough where the planes were, McCallum took off for Watson Lake. Chuck Hamilton loaded me into his plane. It was a two-seater, so he left Al for a later trip. We flew to Airplane Lake where Chuck's partner, Hal Komish, waited with their Cessna. There were several other men there, including a Royal Canadian Mounted policeman. They gathered around when we landed and insisted—over my objections—on carrying me up the steep incline to the Indians' cabin above.

It was a lovely little log cabin just like the one I had imagined living in with my Alaskan Husky. The two trappers greeted us. I looked for Ralph. He was sitting

on the bed at the back of the cabin, looking drawn and
ill. He didn't get up, but when he saw my face in the
doorway, he smiled. I went to him and kissed him.

Ralph told me how he had been found the night
before by the Indian trappers. They had come for him
part way by dogsled and the rest of the way on snowshoes. When Ralph asked them for something to eat,
they had gone back to the sled for food, but had gotten
lost in the darkness. They didn't turn up again until the
morning, but then they had with them a loaf of sour-
dough bread, which Ralph ate. Then the Indians loaded
Ralph onto their dogsled and carried him to their cabin.

Everyone seemed just plain pleased to see me; everyone smiled at me; everyone seemed to want to do something for me. Now the Indian trappers fixed us a meal
of moose steak on crackers and hot tea. I looked at the
food warily, still thinking, This isn't the sort of food I
should eat at first, after so long. My stomach won't be
able to take it. But I nibbled around the edges of the
moose steak and found it delicious. The tea was the best
I ever drank. Not pretend tea this time, but real tea,
flavored tea. I ate the first moose-steak sandwich and
asked for another, and drank another cup of tea along
with it. Normally I drink tea with milk only, but they
gave it to me loaded with Preem and sugar. It was like
drinking glucose.

I held the food all right, but just the process of eating exhausted me. I had to lie down and rest awhile
before I could face the next part of our journey. When

I had rested enough, the men loaded Ralph and me into the back of the Cessna. Chuck and the Mountie, Steve, sat up front.

On the trip in to Watson Lake, Steven kept turning around in his seat and talking to me. He looked like an ad for the Royal Canadian Mounted Police—slim, handsome, fair-haired. It made me feel like a girl again. When he asked me what I wanted right then more than anything else in the world, I told him the simple truth.

"A bath."

It didn't occur to me, heading back for soap and civilization, that it would be another two months before my wish would be granted.

It was still a beautiful day when we landed at the Watson Lake airport that afternoon—the nicest day, I was told, in months. But that night it clouded up and began to snow. It was a terrible storm, a real blizzard. The snowfall completely obliterated Ralph's S.O.S.

XIV

A nurse and driver met the plane at Watson Lake and took Ralph and me by car to the First Aid Relief Station. There is no hospital there, since Watson Lake's year-round population is only about one thousand people (although during hunting and fishing seasons the town draws a lot of tourists). By this time I was exhausted—physically and emotionally. So much had happened in the past twenty-four hours. I remember now that for much of the next few days I was laughing and crying alternatively, and sometimes simultaneously.

At the Relief Station they put me in a room and

began working on me, and I didn't see any more of Ralph for a while. There were a lot of people around, an Associated Press reporter and some local women, and I supposed Ralph had gone off to telephone his wife and children. I peeled off some of my layers of sweaters and pants. Then the nurse took the wrappings off my feet and packed them in bandages. She asked if I wanted a sling for my arm, but I told her not to bother. We were only going to be in Watson Lake for an hour or so before a Canadian Pacific Airline plane was going to make an unscheduled stop to fly us into Whitehorse, where they had a hospital. I'd known all along we'd get back to Whitehorse.

I spent the hour chatting with the women. I felt quite cheerful. The public health nurse accompanied us back to the airport and onto the plane. Now Ralph was with us again, but I didn't get a chance to talk to him because there were so many other people around by this time. The A.P. man went right along with us to Whitehorse. It was only about an hour's flight, and I realized I wasn't even apprehensive about flying in an airplane again. I was pleased with myself about that. An ambulance was waiting for us when we landed. We were then loaded on stretchers and taken to the hospital, where we were put in separate rooms. I remember calling to no one and everyone, as we were carried in, "I'm alive and the world's my home." A little corny, I guess, but I felt fine.

The nurse started preparing me for the doctor's examination, but I asked to stop so I could telephone my mother. When I finally got through to my mother about all I could say was: "Ma, I'm alive!" over and over. Then my mother and I both started crying. Finally I handed the phone to the nurse—her name was Jackie—and she did a little of the talking for me. Then Jackie cut the last pair of trousers off me and gave me glucose and milk and crackers. When she started to wash me, I told her I'd rather take a bath. It was still the only thing I really craved. But Jackie said I couldn't get my feet wet.

I was terribly disappointed. It was such a hopeless task, too, working with a little washcloth and soap on the accumulation of seven week's dirt. Jackie scrubbed and scrubbed. The spots where she actually got through to the skin turned red and peeled. She had stripped me to wash. Now for the first time I saw my body. I was astonished to see how thin I'd become. Underneath all those sweaters and trousers I'd been literally living off my own fat. Now all the fat was gone. I could hardly believe my eyes or the scales when they put me on it. It said I weighed 100 pounds. 100 pounds! Imagine me weighing 100 pounds. I'd lost 40 pounds in forty-nine days. What a great diet I'd discovered!

I wasn't at all happy about my skin. It remained black-dirty despite Jackie's ministrations. When the doctors came to examine me I asked again to be allowed to take a bath, but they refused too. The dirt didn't come off until about four washings later. I stayed in the White-horse hospital for three days and had a complete physical examination. I was found to be in normal condition in all respects with the exception of my feet.

They told me they thought the toes of my right foot would have to be amputated. It was the first time I realized the toes had actually died. I knew it meant a prolonged hospitalization, and I wanted to get home. So I said I'd wait till I got back to New York. The gangrene, being dry, fortunately had stopped at the limits of the injury and not spread into healthy tissue. I was lucky to be so healthy and young or else the infection instead of being confined to one limited area might have traveled up my leg.

From the moment I entered the hospital I was deluged with telegrams, phone calls, fruit, flowers, and gifts from total strangers. Women in Whitehorse I'd never met brought me a pretty robe and nightgowns. I was touched and excited by all the attention. For the first time in my life, I felt like a V.I.P.

On my second day in the hospital my family phoned me. I asked my mother to come to Whitehorse. At first she said she would. Then, after I'd talked to all the rest of the family and she got back on the phone again, she was crying. I asked her what was wrong, and she admitted she was afraid to fly. We agreed that my brother Arthur would make the trip instead. When Arthur asked me what he should bring from home, I said, "Figs, dates, nuts, cookies and halvah."

In a way, I hated to leave Whitehorse. Everyone was wonderful to me there at the hospital and lots of people from town came to visit me. Jackie washed my hair for me, and fed me milk and custard and fruit. Soon I was eating almost normally. I gained five pounds in the three days I was there.

Ralph and I were both astonished by all the reporters and photographers who seemed to be arriving from all parts of the world just to talk to us and take our pictures. People kept offering us money for exclusive stories about our crash and survival. We couldn't get used to the idea that all of a sudden the world was interested in us. It seemed to me a very strange way to become famous: just because we lived. It still seems strange.

Ralph had asked his wife to come to Whitehorse. She and my brother Arthur met in Seattle airport where they waited out bad weather. Arthur told me that, just like the Klabens, the Floreses never gave up hope either. "Ralph is so strong," Mrs. Flores said to Arthur. "And we had so much faith in him."

I wanted to stay in Whitehorse until Mrs. Flores arrived, but she and Arthur decided to take different planes, and Arthur arrived a day ahead of her. Ralph was very disappointed too, because we had talked so often of the two families meeting after our rescue. He had decided to remain in Whitehorse, where he had some Mormon friends he could stay with. Ralph's jaw had healed well, but he needed some dental surgery before he went back home to California.

When I was ready to leave, I went to his room. He

looked so small and shrunken in that white hospital bed. He had lost 58 pounds during our forty-nine days—from 178 pounds to 120. Now that he had been shaven, the scars stood out on his gaunt face. Behind his glasses, the eye above his fractured cheekbone seemed larger than the other.

We talked about my coming out to California to visit him and his family. Then he got very serious.

"Remember what you have to do."

I knew what he meant. My promise to study religion. To be good. To believe in God.

I looked down at him, suddenly realizing I'd spent fifty-three days alone with this man and I didn't really understand him at all. We simply had no channels to communicate with each other. It made me feel very sad.

I leaned down and kissed him. "Goodbye, Daddy-O."

It was the last I was to see of him.

At Idlewild my brother Robby was allowed to come on the plane with the mobile stretcher and attendants. When I saw him I began to cry. The rest of my family and the reporters were all in a waiting room. When the attendants carried the stretcher off the plane, they started to walk right past that room. I saw my mother in the crowd and I cried, "Hey, Ma! Stop, stop; let me see my mother." I was really crying now, but once I'd hugged and kissed my family I was calm. Once I'd seen and held on to my mother, I was all right.

There were a half dozen movie cameras, and flash-bulbs popping and spotlights and reporters and micro-phones. Everyone was shouting questions at me. I had the odd feeling I had done it all before. Perhaps in a dream? I didn't know. But I was not nervous or excited. I was home.

"She's a gift from God," my mother said.

I believed it. How else had I come back?

I was taken to the Harkness Pavilion, a division of the Columbia-Presbyterian Medical Center. The sur-geon examined my foot and told me there was no hope of saving my toes. Two days later they were amputated. The surgeon worked out the "best possible foot" he could leave for me. I was conscious during the operation and only disappointed that they had a screen between me and the surgeon. I kept asking the anesthetist what was happening next. It was very exciting, and not in the least depressing. I was very thankful to be alive and grateful for such expert medical help, and I figured I could get along without a few toes. The operation had to be done in two parts, with the skin grafting later. For skin, they took a nice big patch from my abdomen.

The surgeon told me about some of his patients who have gone through similar operations, and now ski. So perhaps I'll go back to skiing. But the urge to dance has been much stronger with me. I'm thinking of taking ballet lessons to acquire extra good balance.

At first it was thought my arm should be surgically

rebroken and set. But I regained so much flexibility and strength that the orthopedic surgeon decided not to bother. It looks a trifle crooked, but it functions.

My hospital room soon became an office. There were stacks and stacks of letters to answer, and I even had a tape recorder to help me get started with this book. Outside my door was a security guard, so no one could come into see me unless I invited him. I was a celebrity, all right. In a way it all seemed very silly because I was still just the same Helen. But I must admit it was all fun and exciting.

I was back in New York for Passover, not hobbling around my mother's kitchen on crutches, making cookies, as I'd dreamed, but in the hospital where my family came to see me. And I attended Passover services for the first time since I was a child—at the little hospital synagogue, in a wheelchair.

I have heard from so so many people: strangers and friends. People I knew long ago; those I don't know at all—except through their letters, telegrams and telephone calls. I've had letters from Ralph and his daughters, and letters from long-forgotten boy and girl friends. There have been many calls and letters from religious groups, particularly the Mormons. Some nice young Mormon boys visited me in the hospital. I had Ralph's Bible by my bed to show them, and also the little black clock from the airplane, which now works very well.

The thing everyone seems to want to know is what magic ingredient kept us alive, and what have I learned from my experience. I feel kind of like Santa Claus, who gets his letters when they are merely sent to "The Work Shop" or "The North Pole," for since returning home I have received letters addressed to: "Helen Klaben, Brooklyn, New York," and one even to "The Girl Who Survived 49 Days in the Yukon, New York City." I can't get over the fact that the girl is me, Helen Klaben.

Epilogue

There is, of course, no single magic ingredient. I did not survive, as so many newspapers would have it, because of Ralph's strength and his Bible. They were part of it all right, but it wasn't as simple as all that. I'm beginning to think nothing in life is as simple as the newspapers would like us to make out. There were so many strands and elements that, all woven together, enabled me to survive. I now think that everything that happened in my life before the crash, the sum total of all my experiences and relationships, added up to forty-nine days of survival. I believe every experience, every relationship has a meaning and a purpose, even if we cannot understand them, and they are all connected one to another, even if we cannot see the connection.

The first two weeks after my rescue when I was lying in my hospital bed in New York I was burdened with the overwhelming feeling that everyone in the world expected me to have brought back some message from the Yukon about Life and Faith and God. It got so that I even thought I should deliver this message myself. Under this self-imposed pressure and strain I developed severe headaches and, in some ways, suffered more acutely than at any time during the forty-nine days. Looking back on it now, it seems to me that I came away from our second campsite thinking of myself as some kind of saint. I don't know whether I did this to myself, or if Ralph put the idea into my head, or if it was simply public expectation. I know, of course, that I am not a saint; I am not better than anyone else. Usually, I'm not as good. I am still just Helen. I hope I am a better person than I was before; I know I am different.

I learned a lot. I learned—to my surprise—that I did not fear death when it was close to me. That may be because I am young, for when you are young it is hard to imagine your own death, your own mortality. I learned I could control, if not conquer, my fears of darkness and wild animals. I learned that when I set my heart on it I can be as disciplined as anyone. I learned to control my natural impatience when to be patient was the only way to stay alive. I learned that I must stop trying to judge and change people and to accept them as human beings—frail and fallible, like me.

I believe I went through a religious experience out there. No, I did not have a vision, nor did I perform an heroic act, or suffer martyrdom. Those are certainly genuine manifestations of some kinds of religious experience. But there are less sensational kinds. I have strongly believed in God since I was a little girl, and I have spoken to Him as a friend for a long time now. During those forty-nine days I know I experienced God. I know He was with me. I felt His presence—more strongly and clearly than ever before. I know that God put me in the wilderness for a purpose. For a time during those long days and nights it was clear to me why I was there. I admit it is not so clear now, but I think one of the reasons God put me there was so that I could find out much more about myself and my faults.

If anything, I believe in God more fervently than ever before. But I want to make it clear that I have not been converted to anything new or different. I have my faith and I am sticking to it. I certainly do not begrudge other people their faiths and their beliefs. I am still not very happy about many aspects of formal religion. At one time I saw formal religion as one of the causes of social chaos, prejudice, discrimination and intolerance. It was just one more difference between men—thought up by the minds of men, not God—that was responsible for hate and wars and misery. I confess I still feel impatience with sects and artificial groupings. I realize I am too

young and too untrained to argue about theology, but I
know the universal God, the one God for everyone—
whether he be Christian, Jew, Moslem, Buddhist, Hindu
or pagan idolater—must be the same God. If we can
agree there is just one God, why can't we be tolerant of
the many customs and methods of worship? God is,
among other things, good. Goodness, it seems to me,
should be the most important consideration of any formal religion. Let us not confuse ritual with righteousness.

When I was a child, my concept of the universe was
a big giant spinning a lot of little toys—like tops—in a
box. The tops were planets and stars, and there were
little people on them. Every so often the giant would
pick someone off the top and do something to him, and
the giant would laugh and laugh. The giant was some
kind of sadist. It seems to me the Bible sometimes puts
God in the place of my sadistic giant.

But God is kind and good, and if He plucks people
off the planet and takes them away, or if He takes them
from one place and puts them down somewhere else (as
He did to me), then He must have a reason, even if we
can't hope to understand His meaning. If we could understand everything about God, then He would be too
simple, too easy to be God.

I realize that, like everyone else, I make up my own
little dreams about the universe and God and probably
everything else too. I realize I can't now tie all the ends
together; perhaps I never will be able to. For me, there is

a God because I have a personal need for Him. I know some people cannot accept that kind of reasoning or need, but that is the way I feel, that is the way I am. I am also very, very fallible. Despite all my wishes and efforts I see myself slipping back into my old ways—of slothfulness, impatience, gluttony. But I hope I am now more conscious of my failings.

Reading back over everything I have written, I feel that this book is really a personal adventure story, if it is anything at all. So far my life has been an adventure to me; not just my trip to Alaska and the plane crash—all of it. And my adventure is now continuing. I am a student again—at Columbia University—and I see my desire for learning, as well as my efforts to write this book, as part of my continuing intellectual adventure.

Many people have written and said that life is a journey from birth to death, and I think it is too. My journey has just begun, really, but already I think I have found some signposts, some direction signals along the way. Some day my own direction in life will be lighted up for me . . . and I think it may be along some religious lines. Perhaps I'll be able to help God in some way, as He has helped me. For the time being, though, one of the most important signs I have read is: "Don't hurt people." That's one of the things I want to say.

Finally, I want to say that I regard everything that has happened to me in life not as terrible, but as wonderful. Particularly my forty-nine days in the wilderness with Ralph. I owe my life to him, and I learned so much from him—about faith and courage and strength and persistence and endurance. Ralph, for all his limitations as a talker, must surely be one of the most remarkable men in the world. I don't kid myself for a minute that I would have made it down off that mountain alive without him.

All my experiences in Alaska were wonderful. I say wonderful because those experiences enabled me to make a big discovery, an essential discovery. I discovered that God is Love. I discovered for the first time really how much I love my mother and family. I discovered for the first time the emotional transformations and revelations of adult love. I discovered something else I never knew before: I love life. All of a sudden, I see I have a message for the world after all. The message is Love.